Cambridge Elements ≡

Elements in Music and the City
edited by
Simon McVeigh
University of London
Laudan Nooshin
City University, London

URBAN SPECTACLE IN REPUBLICAN MILAN

Pubbliche Feste *at the Turn of the Nineteenth Century*

Alessandra Palidda
Oxford Brookes University

CAMBRIDGE
UNIVERSITY PRESS

CAMBRIDGE
UNIVERSITY PRESS

Shaftesbury Road, Cambridge CB2 8EA, United Kingdom

One Liberty Plaza, 20th Floor, New York, NY 10006, USA

477 Williamstown Road, Port Melbourne, VIC 3207, Australia

314–321, 3rd Floor, Plot 3, Splendor Forum, Jasola District Centre, New Delhi – 110025, India

103 Penang Road, #05–06/07, Visioncrest Commercial, Singapore 238467

Cambridge University Press is part of Cambridge University Press & Assessment, a department of the University of Cambridge.

We share the University's mission to contribute to society through the pursuit of education, learning and research at the highest international levels of excellence.

www.cambridge.org
Information on this title: www.cambridge.org/9781108986779

DOI: 10.1017/9781108981422

First published 2023

A catalogue record for this publication is available from the British Library.

ISBN 978-1-108-98677-9 Paperback
ISSN 2633-3880 (online)
ISSN 2633-3872 (print)

Urban Spectacle in Republican Milan

Pubbliche Feste at the Turn of the Nineteenth Century

Elements in Music and the City

DOI: 10.1017/9781108981422
First published online: August 2023

Alessandra Palidda
Oxford Brookes University
Author for correspondence: Alessandra Palidda, apalidda@brookes.ac.uk

Abstract: At the turn of the nineteenth century, Lombardy and its capital, Milan, lived through a season of intense social and political change, especially in the passage between Austrian monarchy and Napoleonic republics (1796–9 and 1800–2, respectively). While affecting cultural production on all levels, this passage occasioned a significant change in terms of public celebration, with republican festivals and other celebratory occasions hailing from revolutionary France being reframed to suit Milanese specificities. After establishing a solid historical and aesthetic background to Lombardy in this delicate period, to the revolutionary models and to the Milanese substrate, this Element aims to reconstruct and describe the main features of the French republican festivals in Milan, and their impact on the city's landscape, soundscape and self-representation. It will conclude by offering some reflections on these events' consequences on the following century's patriotism/nationalism and cultural production, reinstating them as an interesting, albeit forgotten, case study.

Keywords: public celebration, republican festivals, urban soundscape, urban landscape, Milan,

ISBNs: 9781108986779 (PB), 9781108981422 (OC)
ISSNs: 2633-3880 (online), 2633-3872 (print)

Contents

Introduction

The period ranging from the end of Habsburg rule (1796) to the Congress of Vienna (1814) is an equally interesting and problematic phase in the history of Lombardy. These two decades sit between two proportionally hyper-studied and hyper-celebrated epochs by both historians and musicologists, namely the Habsburg *buon governo* and the Milanese Enlightenment in the second half of the eighteenth century, and the centre-stage role that Milan assumed in the following century in the development and cultural articulation of the Italian nationalistic movement. By contrast, the years considered in this Element, which were characterized by the instability triggered by ongoing warfare, are difficult to label or group in a univocal way. We could attempt a division between a first republican phase (1796–7) and the Cisalpine Republic (1797–9), on the one hand, and, after a thirteen-month Austro-Russian interregnum (1799–1800), a second Cisalpine Republic (1801–2) that soon gave way to the Italian Republic (1802–5) and the Kingdom of Italy (1805–14). Such a division would, however, ultimately be inaccurate because of both the overall transience of political and cultural policies, and the various processes overarching the changes to the political frame. As a result, the scope of any cultural study on this period cannot be defined through labels or years, but rather must be defined through sociopolitical and sociocultural processes. The present Element focuses on public celebration up to the proclamation of the Italian Republic in 1802, when the weakening of the revolutionary impulse within a more tempered frame and the growing personal importance of Napoleon Bonaparte (President of the Italian Republic and later King of Italy) occasioned a structural shift in celebratory practices.

In addition to the proportionally limited attention dedicated to this period per se, cultural production during the Italian republics has suffered from a generalization under the labels of 'occasional' and/or 'propaganda' art. This generalization also affected musical-theatre works, which, despite a keen interest in the seventeenth-, eighteenth- and nineteenth-century Milanese theatrical and operatic landscapes, have seldom or never been the objects of revival, publication or scholarly study. Furthermore, even less attention has been dedicated to the significant body of music produced for public celebration; the extreme scarcity of musical sources (arguably due to the fast pace of consumption, the strong links between pieces and specific occasions, and the controversial political value they embedded) did not make their study easier. In truth, while it is undeniable that much of the music produced on the republican stages retained a strong occasional and political character, it is equally true that the Napoleonic experiences reshaped Milan's musical and theatrical world by either disrupting or accelerating many existing dynamics in terms of audiences, venues, institutions and occasions. It is thus important to study these experiences, both on and off the traditional stages, not just in terms of intrinsic musical value, but also as complex cultural and social phenomena.

A study of sociocultural gatherings with a musical and/or sonorous performative component also offers us the chance for a deeper understanding of Milan's urban musical life, a field that has also suffered from oblivion next to the city's hyper-celebrated operatic scene. The present Element will borrow tools and frameworks from the fertile fields of ethnography, sound studies and urban musicology, approaching the soundscape of Napoleonic Milan as a macrocosmic musical composition resulting from the contribution of numerous performers, and retracing its earwitnesses and living musical practices in the labyrinth of silent sources that characterizes the inquiry on any sonorous object of the past.[1] Sound studies will also help us consider and interpret sonic objects as carriers of complex messages and as powerful forces capable of and aimed at influencing social identity and behaviour.[2] Such approaches have been often under-applied by scholars, who (with notable exceptions) prioritized codified musical components over sonorous/sonic ones, and standardized musical performances over the richness and complexity of the overall soundscape and, even further, sensory experience.[3] By contrast, the soundscape and sonic profiles of urban locations have often revealed a gold mine of information, not only on the city itself but also on its population's cultural horizons, behaviours and sociopolitical and cultural associations.[4] This Element will profit from developments in historical acoustemology and from the broadening of crucial concepts such as those of music making and music makers to explore the musical and sonic experience offered by the Milanese republican festivals and their associated listening and participatory elements, as well as their impact on social and cultural practices.[5]

---

[1] T. Carter, 'The Sound of Silence: Models for an Urban Musicology', in *Urban History* 29/1 (2002), pp. 12–13. C. Bithell, 'The Past in Music: Introduction', in *Ethnomusicology Forum* 15/1 (2006), pp. 4–7.

[2] R. M. Schafer, 'The Soundscape', in *The Sound Studies Reader*, ed. by J. Sterne (New York: Routledge, 2012), pp. 100–1.

[3] D. Fabris, 'Urban Musicologies', in *Hearing the City in Early Modern Europe*, ed. by T. Knighton and A. Mazuela-Anguita (Turnhout, Belgium: Brepols, 2018), pp. 66–8. R. L. Kendrick, *The Sounds of Milan* (Oxford: Oxford University Press, 2002), pp. 3–4.

[4] See, for example, R. Strohm, *Music in Late Medieval Bruges*, 2nd ed. (Oxford: Clarendon Press, 1990), pp. 1–3. S. Schama, *Rembrandt's Eyes* (New York: Knopf, 1999), pp. 311–19. J. J. Carreras, 'Topography, Sound and Music in Eighteenth-Century Madrid', in *Hearing the City in Early Modern Europe*, ed. by T. Knighton and A. Mazuela-Anguita (Turnhout, Belgium: Brepols, 2018), pp. 90–2. F. Nevola, 'Locating Communities in the Early Modern Italian City', in *Urban History* 37/3 (2010), pp. 350–1. P. Canguilhelm, 'Courtiers and Musicians Meet in the Streets: The Florentine Mascherata under Cosimo I', in *Urban History* 37/3, p. 465.

[5] T. Carter, 'Listening to Music in Early Modern Italy', in *Hearing the City in Early Modern Europe*, ed. by T. Knighton and A. Mazuela-Anguita (Turnhout, Belgium: Brepols, 2018), pp. 25–33.

The music and other sonorous components of public celebration in Napoleonic Milan also allow us to enrich frameworks that have often been associated with the city and its cultural production, especially those of political participation and nationalism. With Milan becoming almost synonymous with the Italian nationalistic movement and one of the main theatres of both urban riots and politically informed art, it is important to reframe the origin of both Lombard (later Italian) patriotism and the use of music as a tool of expression and activism within. Such a revision will also contribute a rich case study to ongoing scholarly discourses, namely the problematization of many nationalistic and political/politicized aspects of nineteenth-century Italian culture (especially opera) and the increasingly successful application of the lenses of transnationalism, cosmopolitanism and mobility to cultural and musical discourses.[6] These years also allow some reflection on the element of cultural negotiation embedded in many musical and cultural practices, from the frameworks designed by the French revolutionary theorists to the encounters between Parisian models and local specificities. While the focus will be on the experiences of public celebration and on their impact on the city, some comments on the broader consequences for music and opera production will also be offered. This Element will thus offer a re-evaluation of Milan's republican experiences and will offer a fertile terrain for further historiographical reflection.

Despite the research's focus on music, sounds and soundscapes, most of the primary sources consulted are, as already mentioned, silent and still, for instance chronicles, the press, iconography and administrative documents. The challenge of reconstructing a distant soundscape and musical practices without sonorous evidence allowed a comparative reading of sources that have rarely been included in the historiography of Milanese music or that have been labelled as propagandistic outputs. The description of Milanese events has also been supported by a parallel reading of many French/Parisian sources, which are traditionally more visible and explored. By reconstructing these forgotten or often dismissed experiences sitting at the intersections between political, cultural and historical processes, and between different gazes and sources, we hope to further their understanding not only as complex cultural products but also as a notable, yet still understudied, link in the historiographical chain.

---

[6] See, among many others, the following. A. Körner, 'Beyond *Nationaloper*', in *Journal of Modern Italian Studies* 25/4 (2020), pp. 402–19. A. Körner, 'National Movements against Nation States', in *The 1848 Revolutions and European Political Thought*, ed. by D. Moggach and G. Stedman Jones (Cambridge: Cambridge University Press, 2018), pp. 345–82. R. Parker, 'On Reading Nineteenth-Century Opera: Verdi through the Looking-Glass', in *Reading Opera*, ed. by A. Groos and R. Parker (Princeton, NJ: Princeton University Press, 1998), pp. 288–305. R. Parker, *Arpa d'or dei fatidici vati . . .*, (Parma: Istituto Nazionale di Studi Verdiani, 1997). J. Rosselli, *The Opera Industry in Italy from Cimarosa to Verdi* (Cambridge: Cambridge University Press, 1984), pp. 164–8.

1 Republican Festivals in Northern Italy: Historical and Ideological Background

1.1 Culture and Identity in Lombardy between Two 'Nations'

The turn of the nineteenth century was a period of intense change for Northern Italy, which paved the way for much turmoil and instability, but also for fruitful political reflection. Such sudden and repeated change not only occasioned an increase in the region's political agency but also had a significant impact on its cultural and social geography and on the perception that its inhabitants had of themselves, not to mention the strong consequence on cultural production at all levels. Before delving in detail on the latter sphere, a solid historical, political and social background of these crucial years is necessary.

Given the role that Lombardy and its capital city, Milan, played in the political and cultural dynamics of the Risorgimento, it is tempting to consider them a traditional hub of Italian national sentiment; such a temptation must, however, be scaled down as historically inaccurate. Nineteenth-century histories of Italy and Italian literature, for example those of Sismondi (1804–8),[7] Balbo (1846),[8] Cantù (1865)[9] and De Sanctis (1870),[10] contributed towards the creation of a historiography that saw the foreign dominance on the Italian states as the main reason for the decadence that Italy had experienced throughout the seventeenth and eighteenth centuries. This process, whose starting point was identified in the sixteenth century's political and religious crises, would see its natural conclusion with the Risorgimento, a true rebirth of 'national' freedom, culture and character.[11] Twentieth-century historians such as A. Banti demonstrated, however, that at the turn of the nineteenth century, concepts such as 'nation' and 'independence' were still very far from concretization across the majority of Italian (or even European) contexts.[12] In the case of Lombardy, the only sense of identity was related to the local/regional institutions; it is precisely the events surrounding the Napoleonic republics that triggered a first wave of both political mobility and reflection.[13]

In May 1796, when the French *armée d'Italie* led by Napoleon Bonaparte entered the city of Milan, Lombardy had been a province of the vast

---

[7] J. C. Sismondi, *A History of the Italian Republics* (London: Longman, 1832). Please note that the dates provided in the text relate to when the works were written.

[8] C. Balbo, *Sommario della storia d'Italia dalle origini fino ai nostri tempi* (Turin: UTET, 1860).

[9] C. Cantù, *Storia della letteratura italiana* (Florence: Le Monnier, 1865).

[10] F. De Sanctis, *Storia della letteratura italiana* (Naples: Morano, 1870).

[11] M. Verga, '*Decadenza*', in *Atlante culturale del Risorgimento*, ed. by A. Banti, A. Chiavistelli, L. Mannori and M. Meriggi (Rome: Laterza, 2011), pp. 13–15.

[12] A. Banti, *Il Risorgimento italiano*, 4th ed. (Rome: Laterza, 2004), pp. iv–vi.

[13] N. Del Bianco, *Il coraggio e la sorte* (Milan: Franco Angeli, 1997), pp. 10–12.

multinational Austrian monarchy for almost ninety years. With the exception of the War of the Austrian Succession in the 1740s, the region had experienced a period of uninterrupted peace, stability and economic and cultural growth.[14] Milan had rapidly become one of the brightest centres of the Italian peninsula, with notable advancements in numerous scientific, cultural and social fields, and a cosmopolitan and refined society.[15] Travellers visiting Milan from other Italian states, continental Europe and the British Isles in the central decades of the century reported enthusiastically about the city's grand appearance and flourishing economy, the abundance of cultural and scientific institutions, and its refined aristocracy with an active commitment to civic, cultural and social life and brilliant *salotti* and *accademie*.[16]

Like other provinces of the Austrian monarchy, Lombardy had also been included in the system of reforms of the Habsburg rulers – especially Joseph II (1741–90) and Leopold II (1747–92) – implemented throughout their dominion.[17] As a result, Lombardy had a more centralized government, which aimed at limiting *Ancien-Régime* privileges and institutions, removing unnecessary intermediaries between the State and subjects, and creating a more effective administration.[18] Many of these reforms, especially when the 'enlightened despot' par excellence Joseph II had dealt with issues of religion and local authorities, had generated painful tensions between the Lombard citizens and the Vienna court.[19] Despite these conflicts (many also pacified during the reign of the more tempered Leopold), it was, however, a widespread opinion that the Austrian government had occasioned a very positive effect on a previously lethargic and obsolete

---

[14] See, for example, the following. C. Capra, '*Milano al tempo di Giuseppe Parini*', in *La Milano del Giovin Signore*, ed. by F. Mazzocca and A. Morandotti (Milano: Skira, 1999), pp. 15–33. F. Fava, *Storia di Milano*, vol. 2 (Milan: Meravigli, 1981). G. Gorani, *Storia di Milano dalla sua fondazione all'anno 1796* (Rome: Laterza, 1989).

[15] A. Vicinelli, *Il Parini e Brera* (Milan: Ceschina, 1963), p. 64. M. Canella, '*Aspetti e figure della cultura milanese nel percorso verso la modernità*', in *Il laboratorio della modernità*, ed. by Carlo Capra (Milan: Skira, 2003), pp. 79–81.

[16] C. De Brosses, *Lettres familières écrites d'Italie en 1739 et 1740* (Paris: Perrin, 1885), pp. 95–107. A. Valery, *Historical, Literary, and Artistical Travels in Italy* (Paris: Baudry, 1839), pp. 56–8. A. Young, *Travels in France and Italy during the years 1787, 1788 and 1789*, ed. by T. Okey (London: Dent, 1915), p. 234. R. Sweet, *Cities and the Grand Tour* (Cambridge: Cambridge University Press, 2012), p. 44.

[17] D. Beales, *Enlightenment and Reform in Eighteenth-Century Europe* (London: I. B. Tauris & Co., 2005), pp. 28–31.

[18] S. Cuccia, *La Lombardia alla fine dell'Ancien Regime* (Florence: La Nuova Italia, 1971), pp. 13–18. C. Capra, '*Austriaci e francesi a Milano*', in *Il laboratorio della modernità*, ed. by Carlo Capra (Milan: Skira, 2003), pp. 15–16. D. Carpanetto, *L'Italia del Settecento* (Turin: Loescher, 1980), p. 238.

[19] D. Carpanetto and G. Ricuperati, *Italy in the Age of Reason* (London: Longman, 1987), pp. 227–30.

society. In his *Storia di Milano* (covering Milan's history from its origins to 1792), for instance, Pietro Verri reflected on how Joseph II, although sometimes through hard and unpopular measures, had ultimately pursued his subjects' happiness; his 'enlightened and beneficial' government, continued Verri, 'promoted agriculture and manufactures, and spread education, wealth and prosperity across all social classes. [These were] happy times, then neither completely understood, nor cherished'.[20]

Positive opinions on the Austrian government were still present even in the following century. While visiting Northern Italy in the 1830s, for instance, the intellectual Antoine C. P. Valery (1789–1847) noted how the Austrian government of the Lombardo-Veneto had been visibly beneficial in terms of education, legislation, trade and culture.[21] Even the nineteenth-century philosopher and politician Carlo Cattaneo (a fighter in Milan's Five Days of 1848) notably proclaimed that it was thanks to the Habsburgs that Milan had managed to finally break free from the 'Spanish cadaver' to rejoin the ranks of living Europe.[22] The Austrian government – Cattaneo continued – could not give Lombardy the political prominence of the age of the Sforzas, but it favoured the return to a glorious tradition of productivity and efficiency, with a positive impact on society and culture.[23] The second half of the eighteenth century can be considered the moment when Lombardy rose to become a propelling force for the cultural and political development of the whole country, with Milan assuming the leadership of a gradual process of cultural, moral and social renewal that had started with the dissolution of the Spanish government, and would reach its completion during the Risorgimento. The city became what historians have called 'Italy's watchtower' and 'the modernity workshop': from a drowsy provincial town, Milan turned into a centre of primary importance, found itself at the cutting edge within Italy and developed a strong European vocation.[24]

In 1771, the Lombard capital had also gained further political prominence by becoming the seat of a Habsburg court: following his marriage to the Princess Maria Beatrice of House Este, Archduke Ferdinand Karl (1754–1806), Empress Maria Theresia's fourth-born son, had become governor of Austrian Lombardy,

---

[20] P. Verri, *Storia di Milano* (Milan: Oliva, 1850), pp. 269–79.

[21] Valery, *Historical, Literary, and Artistical Travels in Italy*, pp. 57–8.

[22] C. Cattaneo, *Notizie naturali e civili su la Lombardia*, vol. 1 (Milan: Giovanni Bernardoni, 1844), pp. xciv–xcix.

[23] M. Graziano, *The Failure of Italian Nationhood* (Basingstoke: Palgrave Macmillan, 2013), pp. 44–5. Körner, 'National Movements against Nation States,' pp. 370–2.

[24] R. Schober, '*Gli effetti delle riforme di Maria Teresa sulla Lombardia*', in *Economia, istituzioni, cultura in Lombardia nell'età di Maria Teresa*, ed. by A. De Maddalena, E. Rotelli and G. Barbarisi (Bologna: Il Mulino, 1982), pp. 208–10. Vicinelli, *Il Parini e Brera*, p. 237. Capra, '*Austriaci e francesi a Milano*', pp. 13–14.

and had taken residency in Milan. Even though executive power was concentrated in the hands of government officers such as the *ministro plenipotenziario* (plenipotentiary minister), the presence of an Austro-Lombard court in a city that had not had one since the Sforzas had very strong consequences for issues of culture and identity.[25] In particular, the aristocracy, weakened by Joseph's reforms, reacted positively to courtly life and sociability.[26] Pietro Verri, for instance, commented 'from a provincial city we have become a capital. Now, all oligarchical veneration will be focused only on the monarchy: senators and officers will receive slighter bows, the patron Saints less worship'.[27] The Milanese court was bound to affect the relationship between the Austrian monarchy and Lombardy, creating the new notion of an 'Austro-Lombardian' context, and directly or indirectly affecting all aspects of Milan's social and cultural life.[28]

While many of the reforms implemented by the Austrian government had direct consequences on Milan's functionality (e.g. in terms of public hygiene and lighting), the presence of a Habsburg archduke and his court meant that the city also had to adopt the exterior appearance of a capital, visually mapping out its mutated political and social role.[29] Rising stars of urban architecture such as Giuseppe Piermarini helped redesign many public spaces following the criteria of enhanced practicality and visual harmony. For instance, Piermarini designed or redesigned the headquarters of public institutions (e.g. the palace of Brera), functional spaces (e.g. Porta Ticinese's market square) and Piazza Fontana, the first Milanese square centred on a fountain rather than on a religious or institutional building (Figure 1).[30] After Joseph II's decrees in the 1780s suppressed many religious orders, several buildings were also destroyed or repurposed, with a strong impact on Milan's landscape and its perception: two notable examples are the Swiss Jesuit College (Collegio Elvetico), which became the headquarters of the Austrian government, and the church of Santa Maria alla Scala (the seat of the Imperial Chapel), which was deconsecrated and demolished to make way for the new Teatro alla Scala.[31]

Piermarini also designed the venues representing the court, promoting a sober neoclassical style very different from the Baroque one, and contributing to the

---

[25] Cuccia, *La Lombardia alla fine dell'Ancien Regime*, pp. 19–20. E. Riva, '*La corte dell'arciduca Ferdinando Asburgo Lorena*', in *Il teatro a Milano nel Settecento*, ed. by A. Cascetta and G. Zanlonghi, vol. 1 (Milan: Vita e Pensiero, 2008), pp. 73–4.

[26] G. De Castro, *Milano nel Settecento* (Milan: F.lli Dumolard, 1887), pp. 269–70.

[27] Verri, *Storia di Milano*, pp. 265–8.   [28] Strohm, *Music in Late Medieval Bruges*, p. 92.

[29] Vicinelli, *Il Parini e Brera*, p. 67. Carter, 'The Sound of Silence', p. 13.

[30] A. Scotti Tosini, '*Le trasformazioni della città*', in *Il laboratorio della modernità* (Milan: Skira, 2003), pp. 38–40.

[31] L. Robuschi, *Milano: alla ricerca della città ideale* (Cassina de Pecchi, Italy: Vallardi, 2011), pp. 111–14. See also D. Aspari, *Vedute di Milano* (Milan: n.n., 1792), Plate 15.

Figure 1 D. Aspari, 'Veduta della Piazza Fontana, e Palazzo Arcivescovile' (1788).
© The British Library Board, Cartographic Items Maps 7.TAB.12.

reshaping of Milan's cultural geography. He first expanded the Palazzo Ducale (ducal palace), Ferdinand's main residence in the city centre, and adapted it to the Viennese taste, also reorienting its façade: the building remained in its original location next to the cathedral, but did not face it anymore (Figure 2). In doing this, not only did Piermarini create a residence appropriate to the archduke's rank but he also provided a visible representation of the mutated balance between religious and civic, and old and new, authorities.[32] The architect also curated the project for the *villa reale* (royal villa), the governors' summer residence, erected in the neighbouring town of Monza on the model of Schönbrunn Palace.[33] Like Schönbrunn (and like Versailles, the palace of Ferdinand's sister Maria Antonia), the *villa reale* fulfilled the roles of both summer residence and political-cultural pole, with Monza chosen for various reasons. The town occupied a key position on the road connecting Milan and Vienna and offered a salubrious climate, but it was also symbolically very powerful: its cathedral safeguarded one of the strongest symbols of power in the history of Christian and imperial Europe, the Iron Crown of Lombardy, which Napoleon would also use to declare himself King of Italy in

---

[32] C. Cremonini, *Alla corte del Governatore* (Rome: Bulzoni, 2012), pp. 94–5.
[33] C. Mozzarelli, 'La Villa, la corte e Milano capitale', in *La Villa reale di Monza*, ed. by F. De Giacomi (Cinisello Balsamo, Italy: Silvana, 1999) p. 12. F. Bascialli, *Opera comica e opéra comique al Teatro Arciducale di Monza (1778–1795)* (Lucca: LIM, 2002), pp. 19–20.

Figure 2 F. Durelli, 'Veduta del Palazzo Reale in Milano' (1810).
© The British Library Board, Cartographic Items Maps 12.d.14.

1805.[34] Thanks to the numerous buildings that Piermarini designed, the new style quickly circulated among the aristocracy: many important families had the *imperial regio architetto* (imperial and royal architect), as well as his pupils at the newly established School of Architecture at Brera, design both their Milan residences and pleasure villas.[35]

Piermarini and his school also played a paramount role in the construction of La Scala, Milan's opera house after the Regio Teatro Ducale, the city's only public theatre annexed to the Ducal Palace, burned down in 1776.[36] Its planning and construction were strongly supported by Archduke Ferdinand, who wrote just the last chapter of a long story of cooperation between Milanese citizens and Austrian governors in terms of theatre patronage.[37] A musical-theatre enthusiast (to the point of being reprimanded by his mother for his excessive

---

[34] Valery, *Historical, Literary, and Artistical Travels in Italy*, p. 73.

[35] Scotti Tosini, '*Le trasformazioni della città*', p. 40. Aspari, *Vedute di Milano*, Plate 6.

[36] See the [Ms plan of the Regia Ducal Corte], n.d., I-Mc, Fondo Somma (FS), folder 6. See also K. Hansell, *Opera and Ballet at the Regio Ducal Teatro of Milan, 1771–1776* (Ann Arbor: UMI, 1980), p. 6.

[37] V. Ferrari, *Il Teatro della Scala nella vita e nell'arte* (Milan: Tamburini, 1921), pp. 3–6. A. Palidda, '*Rediviva sub optimo principe hilaritas publica*', in *Music and Power in the Baroque Era*, ed. by R. Rasch (Turnhout, Belgium: Brepols, 2018), pp. 273–80.

interest in artists)[38] and a passionate advocate of local social and cultural needs, the governor tirelessly liaised with the empress to erect a new opera house worthy of his capital, detached from his palace and greater than the Paris Opéra (which he had seen on his travels).[39] The construction of La Scala profited not only from the archduke's support but also from an ad hoc financial partnership between the Vienna court and the Milanese aristocrats; the former sponsored the demolition of the church of Santa Maria alla Scala and the construction of the outer walls and roof, while the latter contributed to the outstanding expenditure in proportion to the boxes they occupied in the Ducale, and received ownership of similar spaces in La Scala.[40]

The theatre was inaugurated on 3 August 1778, winning praise from professionals, audience members and visitors alike thanks to its size, acoustics, décor, stage and functionality.[41] The work chosen for its inauguration, the opera seria *Europa riconosciuta* by Vienna court composer Antonio Salieri, was not only a reference to the strong artistic partnership between Italy and Austria, but also a convincing showcase of the theatre's potential, which reassured the Milanese about their successful investment. While the libretto's dedication acknowledged the governors' support as a necessary condition for the very existence of the theatre, the scenic directions detail a powerful display of both musical and scenic effects, from Salieri's opening storm music to the sceneries of the Galliari brothers and the machines of Paolo Grassi.[42] A second, smaller theatre profiting from similar support and financial partnership was erected on the area of the Scuole Cannobiane (a religious school founded in the sixteenth century by Paolo da Cannobio) and inaugurated a year later (1779) as Teatro alla Cannobiana. The construction of the two theatres represents an important moment in the history of Milan's cultural geography, as these established a first polycentric theatrical system that would gradually expand in the Napoleonic years.[43] The theatres

---

[38] A. Ritter von Arneth (ed.), *Briefe der Kaiserin Maria Theresia an ihre Kinder und Freunde*, vol. 1, (Vienna: Braumüller,1881), pp. 56–63.

[39] See, for example, *Notizie storiche e descrizione dell' I. R. Teatro alla Scala* (Milan: Salvi, 1856), pp. 5–8. Ferrari, *Il Teatro della Scala nella vita e nell'arte*, pp. 10–13. G. Galbiati (ed.), *Il teatro alla Scala dagli inizi al 1794* (Milan: Biblioteca Ambrosiana, 1929), pp. 14–23.

[40] P. Cambiasi, *La Scala 1778–1889: note storiche e statistiche* (Milan: Ricordi, 1889), pp. 345–59. A. Bassi, *La musica in Lombardia nel 1700* (Bologna: Forni, 1992), pp. 74–5. R. Giazotto, *Le carte della Scala* (Pisa: Akademos, 1990), pp. 5–7. [Receipts], I-Mas, Atti di Governo, Spettacoli Pubblici (from now on, AGSP), P.A., folders 35 and 38.

[41] See, for example, the following. P. Landriani, 'Osservazioni sull'Imperial Regio Teatro alla Scala in Milano', in *Storia e descrizione de' principali teatri antichi e moderni*, ed. by G. Ferrario (Milan: Ferrario, 1830), pp. 257–60. Young, *Travels in France and Italy*, p. 234. Valery, *Historical, Literary, and Artistical Travels in Italy*, p. 64.

[42] M. Verazi, *Europa riconosciuta* (Milan: G. B. Bianchi, 1778), pp. 5–6 and 15.

[43] R. Carpani, 'Introduzione', in *Festa, rito e teatro nella gran città di Milano nel Settecento*, ed. by F. Barbieri, R. Carpani and A. Mignatti (Milan: Biblioteca Ambrosiana, 2010), pp. 892–3.

also resulted from a synergy between governors and subjects, the former profiting from a relevant financial contribution and the latter receiving an unusual degree of participation in the management of the opera house: the *palchettisti* (box owners and investors) were in fact deeply involved in the theatre's artistic and financial management.[44] The physical ownership of the theatrical space also had consequences for the theatre-going attitude and practices of the *palchettisti*, particularly in their uninhibited behaviour and strong pursuit of social and entertainment activities.[45] The highest degree of governing authority, embodied until 1796 by the archduke and his family, occupied the so-called *Palchettone* (Great Box), which was as big as a London dining hall (to use Charles Burney's words), sumptuously decorated and positioned in the centre of the tier curve, in the ultimate visible position from both the stage and the hall.[46] Each box was also faced by an antechamber called a *camerino*, which could be used as a storage room and by servants to prepare diversions and refreshments.[47] As Katherine Hansell commented, already at the time of the Ducale, the criticism about the behaviour and listening practices of Italian audiences applied with double force to the Milanese.[48]

Archduke Ferdinand's passion for opera and theatre management was so strong that, in addition to the two new public theatres (which he consistently attended, both alone and with his family),[49] he also built one in his *villa reale*, incurring all of the expenses related to its construction himself and acting as its sole impresario.[50] The Teatro Arciducale di Monza was inaugurated shortly after La Scala, and functioned until late 1795, when the war against France significantly eroded the finances of the Milanese court. Although scantly remembered today, located in a small provincial town and not capable of generating new operatic commissions, the Teatro Arciducale played

---

[44] *Notizie storiche e descrizione dell' I. R. Teatro alla Scala*, p. 9. Giazotto, *Le carte della Scala*, pp. 16–17.

[45] See, for example, De Brosses, *Lettres familières écrites d'Italie en 1739 et 1740*, pp. 422–3. Young, *Travels in France and Italy*, pp. 234–5. S. Romagnoli, 'Il Teatro e "Il Caffè"', in *Economia, istituzioni, cultura in Lombardia nell'età di Maria Teresa*, ed. by A. De Maddalena, E. Rotelli, and G. Barbarisi (Bologna: Il Mulino, 1982), pp. 299–301.

[46] C. Burney, *The Present State of Music in France and Italy*, 2nd ed. (London: T. Becket & Co., 1773), pp. 83–6. R. Bianchi, 'Space and Hegemony at La Scala, 1776–1850s', in *The European Legacy* 18/4 (2013), pp. 733–4.

[47] M. Donà, 'Milan', in *The New Grove Dictionary of Music and Musicians*, ed. by S. Sadie and J. Tyrrell, vol. 5 (London: Macmillan, 1980), pp. 137–8. Bassi, *La musica in Lombardia nel 1700*, pp. 41–3.

[48] Hansell, *Opera and Ballet at the Regio Ducal Teatro of Milan, 1771–1776*, pp. 4 and 159.

[49] Bassi, *La musica in Lombardia nel 1700*, pp. 42–4.

[50] M. Donà, 'La musica a Milano nel Settecento durante la dominazione austriaca' (unpublished typescript, n.d.), NUOVAMISC.A. 0643, I-Mb, pp. 22–3. Mozzarelli, 'La Villa, la corte e Milano capitale', pp. 18–36.

a significant role within the operatic network established between Austria and Northern Italy. A notable example is the 1787 performance of Mozart's *Le Nozze di Figaro*: even though the music was significantly altered, the Monza performance marked the first Italian premiere of a Mozart opera (excluding the juvenile works of the 1770s) during the composer's lifetime.[51] Moreover, this event was immediately followed by a performance of *Le Nozze* at the Teatro della Pergola in Florence, ruled by Ferdinand's older brother and future Emperor Peter Leopold (Figures 3 and 4); it could then be assumed (as Albert Einstein did) that Joseph II, a renowned supporter of Mozart, had recommended the work to his brothers.

Figure 3 Libretto of *Le Nozze*'s performance in Monza (Autumn 1787).
© Biblioteca civica di Monza.

---

[51] A. Einstein, *Essays on Music* (London: Faber, 1958), p. 189. Donà, '*La musica a Milano nel Settecento durante la dominazione austriaca*', p. 23.

Figure 4 Libretto of the performance in Florence (Spring 1788).
© Museo internazionale e biblioteca della musica di Bologna.

The Monza libretto also states that it was thanks to the royal highnesses' personal initiative that the rewriting of the music and the performance took place.[52] Despite the little respect bestowed on Mozart's score, the Italian premieres of *Le Nozze di Figaro* constitute an interesting case study to shed further light on the network connecting Vienna to the main cities of the Habsburg-ruled Italian states, a network that proved particularly efficient in terms of the circulation of musical products.

Ferdinand and his wife, the Princess Maria Beatrice (a highly refined woman and great music patron herself), also hosted regular social and musical events in the Palazzo Ducale, from regular *feste da ballo* (dance feasts) to

---

[52] L. Da Ponte, *Le nozze di Figaro. Commedia per musica da rappresentarsi nel Teatro di Monza l'autunno dell'anno 1787* (Milan: G. B. Bianchi, 1787).

lavish masked balls during the Carnival celebrations, from banquets to *acca-demie* (concerts).[53] These events, often organized with no expense spared, provided the aristocrats with a new cultural and social platform. The patron-age of the governor and his house were even embedded in the decor of the Palazzo Ducale, especially of its public spaces: the portico around the main courtyard, for instance, presented the portraits of the governors of Milan and Lombardy from the thirteenth century onwards, establishing a link between the glorious Sforza Duchy and the present. Similarly, one of the main halls, the *Sala degli Imperatori* (emperors' hall), boasted frescoes (sadly lost in the fire of the Teatro Ducale) depicting the Habsburg emperors.[54] Many events organized at the Archducal Court were also geared towards the creation of a stronger link between the governors and the bourgeois employed in the administrative bodies, who were allowed to enjoy similar sociable rights to the aristocrats.[55]

Starting from the 1770s, Milan could thus profit not only from the positive effects of the Austrian *buon governo*, but also from the presence of governors who brought back the vivacity of a court environment and who behaved as committed patrons of the arts, establishing strong links between themselves and cultural events/venues. Despite his relatively low political agency, Ferdinand was perceived as a natural ally of the Milanese aristocracy in their struggle against Joseph II's centralism in both cultural and political terms; his authority can also be considered to have increased after Joseph's death, and throughout the reign of their brother Leopold II.[56] While the placement of a Habsburg governor in Milan was part of a strategy implemented by the Vienna court to soften the conflict that the centralizing reforms had provoked with the local aristocrats, Archduke Ferdinand was able to forge a particularly positive rela-tionship with his subjects, whose support he returned with a sincere commitment.[57] The young archduke certainly had some detractors (e.g. the historian Giuseppe Gorani, who described him as a profiteer), but the majority

---

[53] See, for example, the [Invoices], I-Mts, SAL 13, SAL 37, SAL 40 and SAL 42, the [*Avvisi*] and [Letters of Invitation], I-Mas, AGSP P.A., folder 5, and Bassi, *La musica in Lombardia nel 1700*, pp. 56–7.

[54] C. Torre, *Il ritratto di Milano* (Milan: Agnelli, 1674), pp. 363–87. See also the *Spiegazione della pianta in cui sono delineati gli appartamenti . . .* (Milan, n.d.), I-Mb, Misc. 1416.E.1, and the [Ms plan of the *Regia Ducal Corte*], I-Mc, FS, folder 6.

[55] See, for example, the [Letter Carlo Albani] (January 1782), I-Mas, AGSP P.A., folder 5.

[56] G. De Castro, *Milano e la Repubblica Cisalpina giusta le poesie, le caricature . . .* (Milan: F.lli Dumolard, 1879), pp. 14–15. C. Capra, '*Milano nell'età delle riforme*', in *Storia illustrata di Milano*, ed. by F. Della Peruta, vol. 5 (Milan: Sellino, 1993), p. 1324. Beales, *Enlightenment and Reform in Eighteenth-Century Europe*, pp. 39–42.

[57] Beales, *Enlightenment and Reform in Eighteenth-Century Europe*, p. 74. C. Cremonini, *Le vie della distinzione* (Milan: EDUCatt, 2012), pp. 44–5. Donà, '*La musica a Milano nel Settecento durante la dominazione austriaca*', pp. 17–18.

of opinions about him were very positive.[58] In early 1772, Pietro Verri commented that the archduke, although he was only 17 years old when he moved to Milan, had learned more about the city in four months than Count Firmian (the plenipotentiary minister) had done in ten years;[59] later that year, when the archducal couple celebrated the birth of their first child, Verri wrote to his brother Alessandro telling him that Lombardy had finally been granted a lineage of 'national' monarchs, and how he rejoiced as a good citizen of Milan while feeling 'Austrian' in his heart.[60] Finally, in the 1780s, Verri commented that the governor '... had obtained the only real success possible for those in his position, namely public esteem and love thanks of his virtue rather than born out of fear or reverence'.[61]

Even the common people seemed to appreciate their governors and their presence: vernacular poems have been found, for instance lamenting the archducal couple's absence during their frequent travels.[62] The governors' legacy did not die out even in the nineteenth century: after the 1814 Restoration, when Ferdinand was already dead, his wife and son, Francis IV, Duke of Modena, visited Milan and were greeted in a surprisingly warm manner, the aristocrats competing for the honour of receiving them.[63]

The feelings of stability and satisfaction brought by the Milanese court were also strengthened by the unsettling news coming from France in the late 1780s and early 1790s.[64] The Milanese aristocracy and high bourgeoisie (traditionally proficient in French and culturally close to their transalpine neighbours) initially showed an interest in the events and debates of the French Enlightenment and Revolution.[65] The extremes of the Reign of Terror, especially its violent critique of governmental and religious institutions culminating in the execution of the French monarchs (Ferdinand's sister and brother-in-law), occasioned, however, a strong conservative switch.[66] While publications coming from the other side of the Alps were automatically burned, the approved newspapers such as the *Corriere Milanese* and *Gazzetta di Milano* were exploited in order to drive the people's mood against the

---

[58] Gorani, *Storia di Milano dalla sua fondazione all'anno 1796*, pp. 130–6.
[59] Hansell, *Opera and Ballet at the Regio Ducal Teatro of Milan, 1771–1776*, p. 101.
[60] Mozzarelli, 'La Villa, la corte e Milano capitale', p. 13.
[61] Bassi, *La musica in Lombardia nel 1700*, pp. 45–6.
[62] De Castro, *Milano nel Settecento*, pp. 274–82.
[63] Riva, 'La corte dell'arciduca Ferdinando Asburgo Lorena', pp. 87–8.
[64] De Castro, *Milano e la Repubblica Cisalpina giusta le poesie, le caricature . . .*, pp. 2–8.
[65] G. Salvi, *Scenari di libertà* (Pisa: Serra, 2015), pp. 14–15.
[66] D. A. Minola, *Diario storico politico di alcuni avvenimenti del secolo XVIII*, ms, I-Ma, vol. 8 (G 118 suss.), p. 37. Gorani, *Storia di Milano dalla sua fondazione all'anno 1796*, p. 382. C. Ingrao, *The Habsburg Monarchy 1618–1815* (Cambridge: Cambridge University Press, 1994), pp. 222–5.

French madmen and their 'tragi-comical' regime, and in support of the valiant imperial troops.[67] A harsh police system similar to the Viennese one was also introduced; accusations of 'Jacobinism' were thrown at people belonging to varied and unrelated backgrounds, including French citizens, Jansenists and academics.[68] Even the Church participated in the general mobilization against the Revolution: parish priests, for instance, encouraged peasants to donate money, enlist and denounce any subversive elements. At the same time, theatres were closed, solemn prayers were recited in the cathedral and churches, and the relics of the patron saints were carried in procession to beseech the protection of God on the Austrian army and against the French 'army of the Antichrist'.[69]

In early May 1796, after barely a month of military operations, the Austrian army suffered a decisive defeat by the French army led by young Napoleon Bonaparte at the Bridge of Lodi, the last bastion on the road towards Milan. When the news reached the Lombard capital, Archduke Ferdinand and his entourage and supporters 'without regrets and without hatred' fled to Maria Beatrice's hometown of Modena.[70] The Milanese citizens witnessed their departure with disbelief and fear, their mood crystallized in these vernacular verses collected by the historian Giovanni De Castro:

> No-one among us can forget
> That unbearable fear, that we all felt
> When we saw the Austrians run away
> All in a rush, leaving us alone.
> Then the Archduke also left,
> And with him gone
> There was no court or soldier left.[71]

While Napoleon marched towards Milan, its inhabitants experienced days of growing panic and uncertainty; even the most committed French supporters such as Gaetano Porro and Galeazzo Serbelloni – future Minister of the Napoleonic police and member of the republican municipality, respectively – did not dare to

---

[67] See, for example, *Il Corriere Milanese* 2/1 (2 January 1794), pp. 6–7; 2/21 (13 March 1794), p. 187; 2/36 (4 May 1794), p. 310; 2/44 (2 June 1794), p. 384; and 2/78 (29 September 1794), p. 662.

[68] Cuccia, *La Lombardia alla fine dell'Ancien Regime*, p. 146. Salvi, *Scenari di libertà*, p. 17.

[69] *Il Corriere Milanese* 2/5 (16 January 1794), p. 53; 2/38 (12 May 1794), p. 334. See also Fava, *Storia di Milano*, p. 8. C. Moiraghi, *Napoleone a Milano: 1796–1814* (Bologna: Megalini, 2001), p. 12. E. Rota, '*Milano napoleonica*', in *Storia di Milano*, ed. by G. Treccani degli Alfieri (Milan: Fondazione Treccani degli Alfieri, 1956), p. 21.

[70] D. A. Minola, *Diario storico politico di alcuni avvenimenti del secolo XVIII*, vol. 8 (G 118 suss.), p. 45, and vol. 10 (G 120 suss.), p. 22. Fava, *Storia di Milano*, pp. 10–12.

[71] De Castro, *Milano e la Repubblica Cisalpina giusta le poesie, le caricature . . .*, p. 60.

step forwards to show their allegiance.[72] As the days passed, republicans and democrats who had been hitherto forced to hide gradually started to come to the fore, while exiles and victims of political persecution flocked to Milan from all over Northern Italy.[73] A particular notable example is Carlo Salvador, a demagogue and gazetteer who had held Jean-Paul Marat's side during the Terror.[74] Salvador gathered around him the most committed Milanese 'Jacobins' and founded Lombardy's first republican club, the *Società degli Amici della Libertà e dell'Uguaglianza* (Club of the Friends of Freedom and Equality), which started to 'prepare' the city for Napoleon's arrival by vandalizing imperial symbols and promoting revolutionary symbols such as tricoloured ribbons.[75] Milan's very first Tree of Liberty was also erected just outside Porta Romana, the city's south-west gate on the way to Lodi, ready to 'welcome' the French army (Figure 5).

Figure 5 C. Vernet, 'Entrée des français dans Milan' (1820).
© Bibliothèque nationale de France.
The Tree of Liberty is visible on the right-hand side.

---

[72] Moiraghi, *Napoleone a Milano*, p. 14.
[73] J. Tulard, *Napoleone. Il mito del salvatore* (Milan: Rusconi, 1989), p. 95.
[74] D. Daolmi, '*Salfi alla Scala*', in *Salfi librettista*, ed. by F. P. Russo (Vibo Valentia, Italy: Monteleone, 2001), pp. 134–5. De Castro, *Milano e la Repubblica Cisalpina giusta le poesie, le caricature . . .*, p. 68.
[75] Fava, *Storia di Milano*, p. 12.

Despite the preparation by local 'patriots', and despite the many enthusiastic depictions in both words and images (most notably, that contained in the opening of Stendhal's *La Chartreuse de Parme*),[76] Napoleon's entry into Milan on 15 May 1796 (Pentecost Sunday), was met with a rather ambivalent attitude. The crowd in Corso di Porta Romana was undoubtedly huge, but more curious than enthusiastic: the few cries of '*evviva!*' came from people who had been paid to give Napoleon a good impression of the Milanese disposition.[77] On the one hand, the young, half-Italian military genius and the radical change he ushered in triggered some earnest curiosity;[78] many, especially among the commoners, were also reportedly intrigued by the French foot soldiers, who were young, badly dressed and badly equipped, but still victorious and joyful, singing the revolutionary tunes that would soon become familiar.[79] On the other hand, apathy and fear were equally widespread among a mostly traditionalist people who could not remember a time when Lombardy had not been a subject of Austria, who were scared of the recent events related to France and who held a positive opinion of their (very) recent governors.[80]

Triumphal or not, the entry of the French army into Milan marked the end of an era: the long and stable Austrian rule giving way to a period of political instability and fast-paced change. All governmental institutions were replaced with new offices modelled on the French revolutionary ones (e.g. the munici-pality and the commune), and even the 'free and independent' *Repubblica Cisalpina* (Cisalpine Republic), established in April 1797 thanks to Napoleon's personal initiative, retained a high degree of dependence from France.[81] At the same time, the new rulers preached a revolution that was understood or invoked by very few.[82] While many of the concepts at the core of the republican creed (e.g. freedom, equality and political participation) were alien *tout court*, the Lombard society, unlike the French one, was not yearning for any sociopolitical change:[83] the aristocracy was not perceived as a burden by the lower strata, and decades of foreign domination and national complacency

---

[76] Stendhal (M.-H. Beyle), *La Chartreuse de Parme*, ed. by E. Abravanel (Geneva: Cercle du Bibliophile, 1969).

[77] Salvi, *Scenari di libertà*, p. 119.   [78] Moiraghi, *Napoleone a Milano*, pp. 15–16

[79] P. Granville (ed.), *Autobiography of A. B. Granville . . .*, vol. 1 (London: Henry S. King, 1874), pp. 16–17. De Castro, *Milano e la Repubblica Cisalpina giusta le poesie, le caricature*, p. 78. S. Pivato, *Bella ciao. Canto e politica nella storia d'Italia* (Rome: Laterza, 2005), p. 10.

[80] Rota, '*Milano napoleonica*', pp. 28–30.

[81] I. Tognarini, '*Le repubbliche giacobine*', in *Storia della società italiana*, ed. by G. Cherubini, vol. 13 (Milan: Teti, 1980), pp. 75–6.

[82] Del Bianco, *Il coraggio e la sorte*, p. 60. E. Pagano, *Il Comune di Milano nell'età napoleonica* (Milan: Vita e Pensiero, 1994), pp. 16–19.

[83] A. Grab, *Napoleon and the Transformation of Europe* (Basingstoke: Palgrave Macmillan, 2003), pp. 153–4. J. Godechot, *La Grande Nation: l'expansion révolutionnaire de la France dans le monde*, 2nd ed. (Paris: A. Montaigne, 1983), pp. 165–6.

had also contributed to a measure of convergence between the different social classes.[84] This attitude, together with a certain local pride and the memory of the recent *buon governo*, made the general disposition towards change and revolutionary concepts rather sceptical; as De Castro commented after surveying vernacular culture of the period, people were instructed to cry out 'Death to the tyrant!', but were not sure whose head had to be chopped off.[85]

Historians recognize that the republican experience played a paramount role in the formation of a cultural and societal base for the later unification movement by challenging traditional authorities and policies, and with the introduction of concepts such as 'nation' and 'constitutionalism'; at this point, a real understanding of such frameworks was, however, limited to the intellectual circles of the aristocracy and high bourgeoisie who had been debating ideas coming from France in the previous decades, and who had been disappointed by the conservative switch of the 1790s.[86] At the same time, the newly instituted freedom of thought and speech attracted many liberals and democrats to Milan from both France and the other Italian states, widening its political basis and enriching the debate within. A particularly active group, destined to become the most radical fringe, came from Southern Italy, mainly from the Kingdom of Naples: a notable example is journalist and playwright Francesco S. Salfi, who was destined to become one of the republic's main cultural activists.[87]

Politics rapidly became the topic of omnipresent debate in both traditional and new formats; political clubs, which, for the first time, were welcoming members from all social classes (including women), sprung up in the weeks immediately following the arrival of the French.[88] Far removed from the 'respectable activists' involved in the clubs and societies of the Habsburg time, these *clubbisti* were often extreme in tone and behaviour, heralding the political change through the violent destruction of the traditional social code: a notable example is the numerous night expeditions organized with torches,

---

[84] A. Bertarelli and A. Monti (eds.), *Tre secoli di vita milanese* (Milan: Hoepli, 1927), p. 427. R. Buclon, '*Napoléon et Milan. Mise en scène, réception et délégation du pouvoir napoléonien (1796–1814)*', PhD dissertation, Université de Grenoble and Università degli studi di Napoli Federico II, 2014, pp. 216–17.

[85] De Castro, *Milano e la Repubblica Cisalpina giusta le poesie, le caricature . . .*, p. 90.

[86] Del Bianco, *Il coraggio e la sorte*, p. 48. Banti, *Il Risorgimento italiano*, p. 16. Salvi, *Scenari di libertà*, pp. 17–20. Buclon, '*Napoléon et Milan*', p. 219. G. Panizza and G. Raboni (eds.), *La Milano di Napoleone . . .*, exhibition catalogue, Milan, Biblioteca nazionale Braidense, 5 May–10 July 2021 (Milan: Scalpendi, 2021), pp. 107–12.

[87] Fava, *Storia di Milano*, p. 20. G. Tocchini, '*Dall'antico regime alla Cisalpina*', in *Salfi librettista*, ed. by F. P. Russo (Vibo Valentia, Italy: Monteleone, 2001), p. 44–6.

[88] A. Ottolini, '*La vita culturale nel periodo napoleonico*', in *Storia di Milano*, ed. by G. Treccani degli Alfieri, vol. 13 (Milan: Fondazione Treccani degli Alfieri, 1956), pp. 402–4. Fava, *Storia di Milano*, p. 16.

flags and loud slogans to disrupt citizens' sleep.[89] The violent hatred towards symbols suddenly identified as 'tyrannical' and 'oppressive', mainly related to the Church and the monarchy, translated into a plurality of violent actions – a 'limitless iconoclastic enthusiasm', to use Nino Del Bianco's words – lacking any clear theoretical grounding.[90] A statue of Ambrose that was reported to have moved, for instance, was chained to a cart and dragged through the streets, while religious practices such as administering of the communion to the sick had to be carried out in secrecy.[91] Even the cathedral's highest pinnacle was saved from demolition (threatened because of the inequality it embodied) thanks only to the placing of a Phrygian hat on the head of its *Madonnina*.[92] These actions were also positively commented on by journalists such as Salfi, who also contributed to their visibility.[93]

With all its excesses, this new 'political atmosphere' was among the most significant novelties associated with the republics, and had a far longer life and greater consequences than their government's actions.[94] Republican and patriotic sentiments had to be directed, however, towards preselected channels that did not threaten the French sovereignty. Napoleon did not trust the Italians' political attitude, which he judged to be immature; furthermore, neither he nor the Directory could allow the dawning Italian nationalism to advocate the establishment of an independent state.[95] While many articles and pamphlets thanked the French Republic for guiding the Cisalpine on the way to democracy 'like a mother who teaches her child to walk', any large-scale initiative of local patriots was received suspiciously, when not harshly repressed.[96] In November 1796, for instance, the proclamation of the Cispadane Republic in Central Italy triggered protests in Milan, with a huge crowd declaring popular sovereignty, and even the drafting of an official act, authenticated by a notary, proclaiming the independence of Lombardy. The French reaction was immediate: the doors of the main patriotic club

---

[89] De Castro, *Milano e la Repubblica Cisalpina giusta le poesie, le caricature*, p. 126. Tognarini, '*Le repubbliche giacobine*', pp. 69–70.

[90] Minola, *Diario storico politico di alcuni avvenimenti del secolo XVIII*, vol. 10 (G 120 suss), p. 30. Del Bianco, *Il coraggio e la sorte*, p. 59.

[91] G. B. Fumagalli, *L'ultima messa celebrata nella chiesa della Rosa in Milano* ... (Milan: Dall'autore contrada del Boschetto, n.d.), p. 11. De Castro, *Milano e la Repubblica Cisalpina giusta le poesie, le caricature* ..., pp. 130–3. Buclon, *Napoléon et Milan*, p. 218.

[92] F. Cazzamini Mussi, *Aneddoti milanesi* (Rome: Formiggini, 1932), p. 20. Fava, *Storia di Milano*, p. 16.

[93] F. Cazzamini Mussi, *Il giornalismo a Milano dalle origini alla prima guerra di indipendenza* (Milan: Famiglia meneghina, 1934), p. 123. N. Parker, *Portrayals of Revolution* (New York: Harvester Wheatsheaf, 1990), p. 14.

[94] Del Bianco, *Il coraggio e la sorte*, p. 60.

[95] Rota, '*Milano napoleonica*', pp. 75–8. Salvi, *Scenari di libertà*, pp. 24–6.

[96] *Discorso sui vantaggi del metodo col quale si è proclamata ... dalla Repubblica Francese la Cisalpina* (Milan: Presso Luigi Veladini in contrada Santa Radegonda, 1797), pp. 4–6. See also the pamphlets in *Giornale storico della Repubblica Cisalpina dall'epoca della sua Libertà e Indipendenza*, ms, vol. 1 (S. Q.+. I. 14), I-Ma, pp. 68–86.

were sealed, the chiefs were arrested and the crowd was dispersed by the military.[97] Similarly, in April 1797, the rumours that the Treaty of Leoben (signed between France and Austria to conclude the War of the First Coalition) would formalise the independence of Lombardy caused a large-scale demonstration of joy in the form of a procession stretching from the cathedral square to the residence of Joséphine de Beauharnais, to whom the crowd offered patriotic hymns and speeches; with the enthusiasm escalating, the Chief of Police had to resolve to using armed force.[98]

The situation was further complicated by the constant friction between the rhetoric of freedom and liberation, and the policies of systematic exploitation implemented since the very beginning of the occupation.[99] Since its inception, Napoleon's Italian campaign had had a more opportunistic than an ideological purpose, namely that of using Northern Italy as a buffer territory and trade currency in future negotiations with Austria;[100] after all, Napoleon had promised his soldiers honour, glory and 'the richest valley in Europe.'[101] Private palaces and public and religious institutions, from the Brera and Ambrosiana libraries to the University of Pavia, were robbed of books, riches and works of art: every day, despite the pleas of intellectuals and artists, convoys loaded with the outcomes of the various spoliations took the road to Paris, where they enriched public galleries and private collections.[102] Meanwhile, the countryside was systematically raided for provisions, crops and anything else that suited the individual battalion commanders.[103] Riots, which were immediately repressed, were already taking place around Porta Ticinese on 23 May (barely a week after Napoleon's arrival). Soon after, villagers revolted and raised the Austrian standard in the rural areas around Pavia, which were ransacked and looted.[104] While the newly established republican newspapers disseminated the (false) news that Archduke Ferdinand had robbed the public treasury before fleeing, and that his ally the King of Savoy had pillaged all of the

---

[97] Fava, *Storia di Milano*, p. 16.

[98] *Giornale storico della Repubblica Cisalpina dall'epoca della sua Libertà e Indipendenza*, ms, vol. 1 (S.Q.+. I. 14), I-Ma, pp. 15–16.

[99] Bertarelli and Monti, *Tre secoli di vita milanese*, pp. 427–8.

[100] Banti, *Il Risorgimento italiano*, pp. 13–14. Godechot, *La Grande Nation*, pp. 76–7.

[101] Cazzamini Mussi, *Il giornalismo a Milano dalle origini alla prima guerra di indipendenza*, p. 118.

[102] Minola, *Diario storico político di alcuni avvenimenti del secolo XVIII*, ms, vol. 10 (G 120 suss.), I-Ma, p. 26. G. Gargantini, *Cronologia di Milano* ... (Milan: Tipografia editrice lombarda, 1874), pp. 283–4. F. W. J. Hemmings, *Culture and Society in France 1789–1848* (Leicester: Leicester University Press, 1987), pp. 77–8. *Annali della Fabbrica del Duomo di Milano dall'origine fino al presente*, vol. 6 (Milan: E. Reggiani, 1885), p. 239.

[103] Moiraghi, *Napoleone a Milano*, p. 17.

[104] Granville, *Autobiography of A. B. Granville*, p. 28. De Castro, *Milano e la Repubblica Cisalpina giusta le poesie, le caricature* ..., pp. 84–5. Buclon, *Napoléon et Milan*, pp. 217–18. O. Sanguinetti, *Insorgenze anti-giacobine in Italia (1796–1799)* (Milan: Istituto per la storia delle insorgenze, 2001), pp. 173–4.

Figure 6 F. Boscarati, 'È questa l'Italia nell'epoca luttuosa della sua prima invasione l'anno 1796' (1814).

© Civica Raccolta delle Stampe 'Achille Bertarelli', Castello Sforzesco, Milan.

churches of Piedmont, the eyewitness Antonio D. Minola reported that, on 19 May, the French emptied Milan's main charity fund without leaving any receipts while the citizens were distracted by a public feast.[105] This multilayered spoliation was evoked in much iconography of the time and in post-Restoration iconography, for instance in an 1814 engraving (Figure 6) in which cockerels symbolising France peck at shattered symbols of traditional authorities, works of art and crops.

Even popular culture reacted to the discrepancy between propaganda and reality, with numerous *bosinade* (short satirical poems) commenting, for instance:

> Freedom, Fraternity, Equality,
> the French on carriages and we on foot.

> Liberty and independence
> until the tolls at the city gates.[106]

---

[105] V. Criscuolo, *Termometro politico della Lombardia* (Rome: Istituto storico italiano per l'età moderna e contemporanea, 1989), vol. 1, p. 82, and vol. 2, p. 298. Minola, *Diario storico politico di alcuni avvenimenti del secolo XVIII*, ms, vol. 10 (G 120 suss), I-Ma, p. 30.

[106] De Castro, *Milano e la Repubblica Cisalpina giusta le poesie, le caricature ...*, p. 81.

At the same time, the pamphlets and journal articles published by the government-controlled media presented a new historiography of (Northern) Italy, which linked the glorious epochs of Ancient Rome, the Lombard League and the Sforzas to the newly found 'national' freedom and the 'fair' phase of history initiated by the French: a common purpose between Cisalpine and French patriots was, however, virtually non-existent.[107]

While the strongest supporters of the former regime had left Milan, the new government offices included some of the most prestigious citizens, such as Pietro Verri and Giuseppe Parini, which promoted a link between the French revolutionaries and the champions of the Milanese Enlightenment; they were presented as heralds of the ongoing political and cultural renaissance.[108] In truth, neither Verri nor Parini could tolerate the degeneration of political communication: both attended the meetings of the municipality, but withdrew after a short while, leaving embittered writings on the government's hypocrisy.[109] Verri, an experienced journalist and founder of the celebrated periodical *Il Caffè*, published some articles on Salfi's *Termometro politico della Lombardia*, but these were heavily revised and misinterpreted.[110] Parini, who had used poetry as a weapon of social critique, produced a short poem entitled *Il ciarlatano* (*The Charlatan*), which provided a pitiless caricature of the new regime, as opposed to enlightened reformism:

> A *philosophe* comes
> All humble, and says
> 'One step at the time,
> Slowly, . . . we want
> To purge morals from mistake
> Therefore, everybody must improve
> Himself first, then the others.
>
> Here comes another one, screaming:
> 'The whole world is corrupted.
> We have to overthrow
> The laws and government.

---

[107] See, for example, the 'Rapporti letti nella pubblica sessione della Società di Pubblica Istruzione ed Arti in Milano nel giorno 29 Ventoso A.V RF' (19 March 1797), in *Giornale storico della Repubblica Cisalpina dall'epoca della sua Libertà e Indipendenza*, ms, vol. 1 (S.Q.+. I. 14), I-Ma, pp. 4–11.

[108] Criscuolo, *Termometro politico della Lombardia*, vol. 1, pp. 81–5. See also the 'Dialogo tra Nova e Verri di ritorno dagli Elisi' in *Il giornale senza titolo*, 46 (Milan: n.n., 1798), pp. 186–7. Tulard, *Napoleone*, p. 95. Moiraghi, *Napoleone a Milano*, p. 16.

[109] Cazzamini Mussi, *Aneddoti milanesi*, p. 94. A. Bosisio, *Storia di Milano* (Milan: Giunti-Martello, 1958), pp. 289–91.

[110] Criscuolo, *Termometro politico della Lombardia*, vol. 1, pp. 29–30.

We can save it only with my creed,
Everything else is futile.'
Watch out for the latter: he is a charlatan.[111]

Many aristocrats traditionally involved in local administration and politics were excluded from public office, and even arrested for conspiring against the revolution and the people, which deeply shocked many.[112] Executive power was concentrated in the hands of a few French commissioners and General Hyacinthe F. J. Despinoy, *Comandante della piazza* (chief-in-command) of the battalions of the Armée d'Italie stationed in Milan; the latter became renowned for his arrogance and was nicknamed *Generale ventiquattro ore* (the twenty-four-hours general) due to his inflexibility regarding the timely execution of his orders.[113]

While leading to an increase in illusions and disappointments alike, the French conquest pervaded Milan with a surge of cultural and political renewal: interestingly, both the Habsburg reforms and the republics' radical debate made Lombardy a notable example of innovation and modernity, and a powerhouse for both political debate and cultural production. In the unstable republican years, rulers had to take stronger steps in order to secure, control and direct the people's mood, conceal the opportunistic purposes embedded in the occupation of Lombardy and carefully craft and manoeuvre a non-existent 'republican' and 'Italian' patriotism. It was, indeed, a very delicate mission, for which control of the performing arts and public spectacle assumed paramount importance.

1.2 Public Feasts and Spectacles in Lombardy: An Overview

Celebratory events organized in republican Milan to serve the needs of its new government were not created *ex novo*; instead, they repurposed and reused several pre-existent elements.[114] Ironically, although republican propaganda advocated the erasure of all pre-revolutionary symbols (the very concept of *Ancien Régime* being theorized by revolutionary thinkers to support the idea of radical change),[115] some of the republican festivals' elements can be directly linked to the traditional celebration of religious and civic authorities. This section will thus present an overview of public

---

[111] G. Parini, *Poesie* (Florence: Barbera, 1808), pp. 397–8.

[112] De Castro, *Milano e la Repubblica Cisalpina giusta le poesie, le caricature . . .*, p. 85.

[113] Grab, *Napoleon and the Transformation of Europe*, p. 154. Moiraghi, *Napoleone a Milano*, p. 17.

[114] E. Balmas, '*Dalla festa di corte alla festa giacobina*', in *Lo spettacolo nella Rivoluzione francese*, ed. by P. Bosisio (Rome: Bulzoni, 1989), pp. 140–4.

[115] W. Doyle, 'Introduction', in *The Oxford Handbook of the Ancien Régime*, ed. by W. Doyle (Oxford: Oxford University Press, 2011), pp. 1–5.

spectacles and celebratory events in Austrian Lombardy, establishing part of the frame in which the Parisian model, described in the next section, was transplanted.

Milan's tradition of public celebration, entertainment and spectacle was long standing and varied, the city having been a major religious centre (the seat of the Ambrosian Church and a Counter-Reformation powerhouse) and a political and financial capital for several centuries.[116] As a result, the city boasted a stratified society with different entertainment and sociable needs, and a multilayered celebratory culture. Similarly to many other coeval cities, the majority of public celebrations, called *pubbliche allegrezze* (public rejoicings), were linked to religious, civic or political referents, and were organized according to a ritual that highlighted the links between their object/organizer and the community.[117] Many of these occasions are difficult to label as theatrical performances, feasts or rituals: Roberta Carpani noted, for instance, that, in this context, terms such as *festa* (festival/feast), *rito* (ritual/rite) and *teatro* (theatre/performance) define unstable and overlapping labels that need to be reconsidered case by case. What is certain is that public celebrations and spectacles informed the shared perception of time and space, constituting a defining element of Milan's identity and geography.[118]

Milan's celebratory culture was deeply informed by religion, rooted in the shared time and space: the city followed the calendar of holidays dictated by the Ambrosian Church, as well as by the different religious orders, while the urban geography was modelled on religious buildings, from the central cathedral to the ubiquitous churches, convents and schools. Even the theatrical calendar, with its hierarchical system of seasons, was heavily modelled on the Ambrosian calendar.[119] Milan's strong Counter-Reformation legacy also encouraged both heartfelt personal devotion and participation in communal rituals: religious life in eighteenth-century Milan could almost be described as a civic duty.[120] At the

---

[116] Valery, *Historical, Literary, and Artistical Travels in Italy*, pp. 38–9. P.-J. Grosley, *Observations sur l'Italie et les Italiens*, vol. 1 (London: n.n., 1770), p. 184. De Brosses, *Lettres familières écrites d'Italie en 1739 et 1740*, pp. 94–5. Burney, *The Present State of Music in France and Italy*, pp. 79–80.

[117] G. D'Amia, 'La città fatta teatro: apparati effimeri ed "embellissement" urbano …', in *Il teatro a Milano nel Settecento*, ed. by A. Cascetta and G. Zanlonghi, vol. 1 (Milan: Vita e Pensiero, 2008), pp. 97–8.

[118] Carpani, '*Introduzione*', pp. 892–5.

[119] M. Feldman, *Opera and Sovereignty. Transforming Myths in Eighteenth-Century Italy* (Chicago: The University of Chicago Press, 2007), pp. 144–7.

[120] P. Vismara, '*Forme di devozione e vita religiosa tra continuità e rinnovamento*', in *Il teatro a Milano nel Settecento*, ed. by A. Cascetta and G. Zanlonghi, vol. 1 (Milan: Vita e Pensiero, 2008), pp. 57–9. P. Vismara, '*Il sistema della religione cittadina dei milanesi nel Settecento …*', in *La cultura della rappresentazione nella Milano del Settecento*, ed. by R. Carpani, A. Cascetta and D. Zardin (Rome: Bulzoni, 2010), pp. 45–7.

same time, the most prestigious occasions could reach levels of splendour and theatricality that harked back to Baroque practices and that attracted members of the community and visitors alike.[121] Many celebrations also included a refined musical accompaniment, which often blended the traditional Church style with a more compositional and performative one, closer to the repertoires heard in chamber-music concerts and in the opera house.[122] The Church also provided an important platform for the meeting of the religious and civic/ political authorities: while many members of the court and government (e.g. Princess Maria Beatrice) were renowned for their devotion, many occasions saw the ritualized participation of the highest government authorities in liturgical and para-liturgical moments. From the main holidays to the Te Deum sung in conjunction with current events (warfare, epidemics, deaths, appointments of new bishops and cardinals, etc.), religious celebrations saw the juxtaposition of secular and religious authorities, symbols and figures.[123]

At the same time, events and figures related to the governing authority (long before the establishment of Ferdinand's court) triggered both civic and religious/liturgical celebrations of surprising complexity, which took place in both churches and public spaces. In 1739, for instance, the visit of (still) Archduchess Maria Theresia occasioned five days of complex festivities, which involved liturgical and para-liturgical celebrations (e.g. solemn masses and religious processions), events in a court-like setting (e.g. banquets and *feste da ballo*), military parades, general illumination, theatrical performances and lavish fireworks.[124] Similarly, in 1747, the birth of Archduke Leopold was celebrated with both solemn masses and appositely composed cantatas in the city's main churches, and with a theatrical performance followed by a grand *festa da ballo* in the Teatro Ducale, appositely refurbished, lit and decorated.[125] Finally, in

---

[121] *Notizie storiche e descrizione dell' I. R. Teatro alla Scala*, pp. 6–7. Grosley, *Observations sur l'Italie et les Italiens*, p. 115. De Brosses, *Lettres familières écrites d'Italie en 1739 et 1740*, pp. 82–90. Vismara, '*Forme di devozione e vita religiosa tra continuità e rinnovamento*', pp. 61–2.

[122] Burney, *The Present State of Music in France and Italy*, pp. 80–1. F. Degrada, '*Le esperienze milanesi di Mozart*', in *L'amabil rito*, ed. by G. Barbarisi, C. Capra, F. Degrada, et al., vol. 2 (Bologna: Cisalpino, 2000), pp. 734–5. A. Palidda, '*Exsultate, jubilate: musica sacra?*', in *La nostra musica da chiesa è assai differente*, ed. by C. Toscani and R. Mellace (Lucca: SEdM, 2018), pp. 216–17.

[123] Vismara, '*Il sistema della religione cittadina dei milanesi nel Settecento …*', p. 46. D. Costantini and A. Magaudda, 'Feste e cerimonie con musica nello Stato di Milano', in *Seicento inesplorato. L'evento musicale tra prassi e stile: un modello di interdipendenza*, ed. by A. Colzani, A. Luppi and M. Padoan (Como: A.M.I.S., 1993), p. 83.

[124] A. Mignatti, *Scenari della città* (Pisa: F. Serra, 2013), pp. 47–65.

[125] De Castro, *Milano nel Settecento*, pp. 177–8. Bertarelli and Monti, *Tre secoli di vita milanese*, p. 297. F. Barbieri, R. Carpani and A. Mignatti (eds.), *Festa, rito e teatro nella gran città di Milano*, exhibition catalogue, Milan, Pinacoteca Ambrosiana, 24 November 2009– 28 February 2010 (Milan: Biblioteca Ambrosiana, 2010), pp. 915–19.

September 1771, Archduke Ferdinand's journey from Vienna to Milan to meet his bride-to-be was celebrated with a lavish procession led by the canons of S. Ambrogio.[126]

On many occasions, especially with attendance by notable figures, celebrations went significantly beyond the borders of dedicated venues and included a geographical narrative that unfolded in the public space. On these occasions, the urban space had to be 'sacralised' (i.e. removed from its daily connotations) and projected into the spheres of the extraordinary and magnificent.[127] This was accomplished through decoration, illumination, the construction of temporary apparatuses and structures, and forms of public charity and entertainment.[128] The events organized in Milan to celebrate royalty prior to the establishment of a local court can be considered particularly lavish, as they needed to 'present' royals to their people in absentia: the scale and decor of apparatuses often matched and even surpassed that of theatrical performances.[129] In 1716, for instance, the birth of Emperor Charles VI's heir Leopold Johann was celebrated with wine fountains and colossal firework machines, while complex structures were erected to solemnize the entries of the Archbishops Stampa (1739) and Pozzobonelli (1744).[130] The Wars of Spanish and Austrian Successions and the more sober taste advocated by Emperor Charles VI had already occasioned a reduction of the (secular) festive apparatuses, while Maria Theresia and her children applied principles of rationalization and centralization. This meant reducing the autonomy of many civic bodies, shifting the focus of public festivities closer to the ruler and carefully controlling all detail within the actual celebrations. A notable example is the plethora of documents aimed at regulating general behaviour both inside and outside public venues in order to discipline public entertainment and avoid disorder.[131]

Some traditional elements, appositely repurposed and carefully controlled, were retained in arguably the most representative public celebration of Austrian Lombardy, that for the wedding of Ferdinand of Habsburg and Maria Beatrice of Este in 1771. The wedding held a deep symbolic meaning, completing a refined

---

126 Gargantini, *Cronologia di Milano* ..., p. 271.
127 Feldman, *Opera and Sovereignty*, pp. 152–3.   128 D'Amia, '*La città fatta teatro*', p. 98.
129 A. Mignatti, 'Magnificence and Regality in Milanese Celebratory Sets . . .', in *Magnificence in the Seventeenth Century*, ed. by G. Versteegen, S. Bussels, and W. Melion (Leiden: Brill, 2021), pp. 276–7. Vismara, '*Il sistema della religione cittadina dei milanesi nel Settecento . . .*', pp. 51–2.
130 T. Ceva, *Relazione delle pubbliche feste fatte dalla città di Milano alli 7 di giugno 1716* (Milan: G. P. Malatesta, 1716), pp. 25–32. D'Amia, '*La città fatta teatro*', p. 100. Barbieri, Carpani and Mignatti, *Festa, rito e teatro nella gran città di Milano*, pp. 912–13. Mignatti, *Scenari della città*, pp. 89–99.
131 Feldman, *Opera and Sovereignty*, pp. 141–3. See also the [Documents] in I-Mas, AGSP P.A., folders 1, 4 and 5, and in I-Mc, FS, folder 1.

dynastic plan and occasioning the establishment of the Milanese court: as a result, the empress, who was usually rather thrifty when it came to entertainment, incurred all expenses.[132] A complex programme of celebrations was devised to take place over fifteen days, making use of the city's different spaces and forces. On the one hand, the most renowned Milanese artists were appointed to many of the tasks needed, from Piermarini, who redecorated the public space and designed the temporary apparatuses, to Parini, who compiled the official chronicle of the celebrations and wrote the libretto for the *festa teatrale Ascanio in Alba*.[133] The music for the two large-scale works performed in the Teatro Ducale, on the other hand, was supplied by composers directly linked to Vienna: *Il Ruggiero* was composed by Johann Adolph Hasse (one of Maria Theresia's favourites) on a libretto by the court poet Metastasio, while *Ascanio in Alba* was entrusted to the Austrian prodigy Mozart, specifically chosen by the empress in concert with Count Firmian.[134]

The *Giornale delle feste*, the celebrations' official programme, details different occasions that brought together urban traditions (e.g. the masked procession of the *facchini* or porters), aristocratic pastimes (e.g. the banquets at the Ducal Palace and the carriage parade with a background of instrumental music), popular entertainment (e.g. horse races and greased poles) and public demonstrations of goodwill.[135] A notable example is that of the *Banchetto delle Spose* (the brides' banquet), which took place in the public gardens in the Corso di Porta Orientale. The gardens had been appositely redecorated by Piermarini so that they resembled a majestic dining hall surrounded by arches made of weaved branches, leaves and flowers (Figure 7).[136]

There, the archducal couple distributed a dowry and a silver medal with their depiction to 220 brides of humble conditions, and shared with them and their husbands a lavish meal accompanied by music; the event also became a spectacle, observed by hundreds of attendees thanks to the benches provided.[137] The atmosphere of idyllic communality, also referenced in *Ascanio in Alba*'s allegorical pastoral setting, forged a link

---

[132] M. Donà, *Ascanio in Alba* (Lucca: LIM, 1997), pp. 7–8. K. Hansell, *Opera and Ballet at the Regio Ducal Teatro of Milan, 1771–1776*, pp. 18–21. De Castro, *Milano nel Settecento*, p. 254.

[133] Barbieri, Carpani and Mignatti, *Festa, rito e teatro nella gran città di Milano*, pp. 923–4.

[134] Degrada, 'Le esperienze milanesi di Mozart', pp. 737–8. C. Wysocki, '*Il giovane Mozart e il Conte Firmian*', in *Mozart e i musicisti italiani del suo tempo*, conference proceedings, Rome, 21–2 October 1991, ed. by A. Bini (Lucca: LIM, 1994), p. 87.

[135] *Giornale delle feste* (1771), I-Mb, Misc. 1416.D13. G. Parini, *Descrizione delle feste celebrate in Milano per le nozze delle LL. Altezze Reali* ... (Milan: Società tipografica de' Classici Italiani, 1825), pp. 32–3. Bassi, *La musica in Lombardia nel 1700*, p. 149. Donà, *Ascanio in Alba*, p. 13.

[136] De Castro, *Milano nel Settecento*, p. 255.

[137] Parini, *Descrizione delle feste celebrate in Milano per le nozze delle LL. Altezze Reali*, pp. 7–13.

Figure 7 G. C. Bianchi, 'Sala verde e Banchetto' (1771).
© Civica Raccolta delle Stampe 'Achille Bertarelli', Castello Sforzesco, Milan.

between the placement of the new governors and the dawning of an age of prosperity for Lombardy, also stressing concepts at the core of the Habsburgs' governmental doctrine, such as those of *buon governo* and *pubblica felicità*.[138]

The performances in the Ducale, continuing throughout the celebrations, presented similar imagery and concepts. *Ascanio* contained – to use Parini's words – a 'perpetual allegory' of the archducal wedding, blessed by the empress as Venus and establishing a royal dynasty destined to last forever. Similarly, *Il Ruggiero* exalted the bravery and kindness shown by an ancestor of the House Este in the times of Charlemagne.[139] The Teatro Ducale had also been appositely redecorated by resident scenographers, the Galliari brothers, who had also produced a new painted curtain portraying the wedding of Telemachus.[140] Finally, the celebrations included occasions for the aristocracy to enter the Ducal Palace and share meals, musical performances and entertainment with

---

[138] Cremonini, *Alla corte del governatore*, pp. 98–9. Degrada, '*Le esperienze milanesi di Mozart*', p. 742. D'Amia, '*La città fatta teatro*', p. 122.

[139] Parini, *Descrizione delle feste celebrate in Milano per le nozze delle LL. Altezze Reali*, pp. 17–21. See also the closing chorus in Donà, *Ascanio in Alba*, p. 43, and the 'Licenza' in P. Metastasio, *Il Ruggiero ovvero L'eroica gratitudine* (Rome: N. Barbiellini, 1771), pp. 60–1.

[140] Parini, *Descrizione delle feste celebrate in Milano per le nozze delle LL. Altezze Reali*, pp. 14–15.

the archducal couple, establishing their presence and residence as the new catalysts of social and cultural life.[141]

Many of these elements of public celebrations (e.g. the modification of the urban space through temporary structures, the rich symbolic thread connecting events inside and outside traditional venues and the offering of entertainment and charity to the lower classes) were actively reused within the frame of republican festivals. The juxtaposition of familiar frameworks with new and mostly alien concepts and symbols generated a very idiosyncratic, yet dynamic, experience, which also had strong consequences for how Milan perceived itself and performed as the capital of a new republican state. Some considerations of the Parisian model of republican festivals are now necessary in order to fully understand and explore this complex, multilayered experience.

1.3 The French Republican Festivals: Theory and Practice

Republican festivals (i.e. large-scale gatherings organized and offered by governmental institutions to celebrate a particular event, figure or concept related to the revolutionary creed or narrative) played a paramount role within the plan devised in order to impress, educate and guide the new, republican people of Milan. Both chronicles and archival documents suggest that forms of republican celebration – ranging in scale from semi-spontaneous gatherings fuelled by the local 'patriots' to large, highly structured festivals organized by governmental commissions – were a constant in the republican years. The conception and main features of republican festivals have already been the object of a well-established, mainly French, scholarship; it will be enough to provide a recap here on a few particularly relevant issues.

Festivals were supported by a rigorous theoretical underpinning, which originated in the second half of the eighteenth century in the works of Jean-Jacques Rousseau, and was furthered through their re-elaboration by some notable personalities of the French Enlightenment and Revolution, such as D'Alembert, Diderot, Voltaire and Robespierre. One of their main reflections had been that on morally healthy spectacles to be included within a plan of public education; this had led to a sharp critique of theatre, which was seen as an aristocratic and corrupted ritual where any spontaneous participation was lost.[142] While theatre underwent a long process of restructuring that turned it from a merely hedonistic or academic pastime to a privileged moment of civic

---

[141] Parini, *Descrizione delle feste celebrate in Milano per le nozze delle LL. Altezze Reali*, pp. 23 and 44. De Castro, *Milano nel Settecento*, p. 256.

[142] S. Ferrone, '*La danse fut suspendue* . . .', in *Lo spettacolo nella Rivoluzione francese*, ed. by P. Bosisio (Rome: Bulzoni, 1989), pp. 35–6.

maturation, the need remained for innovative and educational forms of social and cultural gathering.[143]

This was also supported by the growing importance of the concept of public opinion, perceived as an entity powerful enough to justify the large-scale mobilisation of public administration and funds.[144] According to republican theorists, there could be no better place for the development of a new, positive public opinion than regenerated France and its sister republics. Here, public opinion could flourish anew, steered by the civic-minded *gens des lettres* and parliamentary forces, and guide the masses on the path towards the nation's greatness. This renewal was framed within a wider project entrusting revolutionary France with historical responsibility for a total regeneration of society, which had to be run by *hommes nouveaux*, hence the constant stress on the 'new', 'renewed' and 'regenerated'. This utopian renewal of both the individual and the people (or their return to an uncorrupted state of innocence) constituted one of the Revolution's main ideals, and was supported by a strong activism, hence the explosion of social practices aimed at breaking with the past through the constant realization of the revolutionary ideology, embedded in rhetorical gestures, symbols, and individual and collective actions.[145] This active repetition provided the new politically active class with structure and unity, and made them the heroes of their own, constantly performed, epic: it is not the case that the rhetoric of the festivals was often fervent and ritualized, and embedded a dramatic, even tragic, component.[146]

To replace the corrupted theatrical performances, Rousseau had proposed the public festivals that took/taking place in smaller, rural communities: far away from the morally degraded cities, these occasions saw the whole community gathering spontaneously and celebrating shared values.[147] This idyllic countryside became a constant presence in the imagery of the republican festivals, with the Tree of Liberty harking back to a world of traditional rites, as well as repurposing the traditional referencing to a mythical golden age.[148] Bound together in this intimately felt celebration, the people realized the participation in public life that, according to the theory of the *contrat social*, constituted the basis of society.[149] During these celebrations, as opposed to the feigned

---

[143] P. Bosisio, '*Introduzione*', in *Lo spettacolo nella Rivoluzione francese*, ed. by P. Bosisio (Rome: Bulzoni, 1989), pp. 7–8.

[144] M. Ozouf, *L'homme régénéré* (Paris: Gallimard, 1989), pp. 21–3.

[145] Ozouf, *L'homme régénéré*, pp. 32–6 and 116–19. L. Hunt, *Politics, Culture, and Class in the French Revolution*, 2nd ed. (London: Methuen & Co., 1986), pp. 12–14.

[146] Hunt, *Politics, Culture, and Class in the French Revolution*, pp. 36–7.

[147] C. Pancera, '*Feste e rituali della rivoluzione*', in *Europa 1700–1992. Storia di una identità*, vol. 2 (Milan: Electa, 1991), pp. 164–7.

[148] O. Ihl, *La fête républicaine*, ed. by M. Ozouf (Paris: Gallimard, 1996), pp. 241–2.

[149] M. Ozouf, *La fête révolutionnaire: 1789–1799* (Paris: Gallimard, 1976), pp. 238–40.

emotions recreated by actors, people exteriorized their true feelings; republican feasts adopted spectacular/theatrical tools, but always demanded the active participation of their attendees, especially those traditionally excluded from the cultural rituals of the elite.[150] The people assembled within these events could thus rejoice in celebrating themselves, triggering the '*contemplation des citoyens par eux mêmes*' (self-contemplation) that both Rousseau and Robespierre described as 'the greatest of all spectacles'.[151] These immense gatherings, bringing together people of all social classes, made everything 'old' and 'partial' fade away, and became rites as sacred as those performed in front of church altars, embodying the regeneration brought by the Revolution.[152]

As was the case with other/older forms of public celebrations, several tools used in republican festivals for both exaltation and entertainment were tightly linked to theatre and other performing arts; many celebratory moments within the festivals could indeed be considered full-scale theatrical performances or spectacles.[153] As a result, republican festivals caused the very concepts of 'theatre' and 'feast' (already described as problematic labels when dealing with public festivities) to draw closer;[154] the borders between organized performance and (allegedly) spontaneous celebration were intentionally blurred. At the same time, republican festivals advocated the weakening or elimination of the divisions between actors, subject matter and audience, with this merging process recognized as a defining feature of the urban cultural landscape in both republican France and its sister republics.[155] Theatre scholars observed a return of these public spectacles to an almost pre-Renaissance status, when the divisions between organized performances, urban spectacles, and secular and religious ceremonies were not particularly sharp.[156]

While traditional performance venues were also exploited, the revolutionary spectacle par excellence took place en plein air, in the streets and squares of the 'liberated' cities and around the new republican symbols: both theatre's elitist matrix and its corrupted emotions were thus overcome, while the richness of pre-existing experiences provided a plethora of reusable features. Given their importance not only as tools of public education, but also as instruments of

---

[150] F. Mastropasqua, *Le feste della Rivoluzione francese: 1790–1794* (Milan: Mursia, 1976), pp. 18–19. Bosisio, '*Introduzione*', p. 9.

[151] M. Robespierre, *Rapport fait au nom du Comité de salut Public ... sur les Fêtes nationales* (Paris: Quiber-Pallissaux, 1793), p. 2.

[152] J. Michelet, *Histoire de la Révolution française*, vol. 2 (Paris: Chamerot,1847), pp. 167–8.

[153] Balmas, '*Dalla festa di corte alla festa giacobina*', pp. 137–40.

[154] Carpani, '*Introduzione*', pp. 892–5.

[155] Ozouf, *La fête révolutionnaire*, pp. 238–40. Feldman, *Opera and Sovereignty*, pp. 153–4.

[156] Ferrone, '*La danse fut suspendue ...*', pp. 29–30. P. Bosisio, '*Un poeta al servizio di un nuovo modello di spettacolo*', in *Vincenzo Monti nella cultura italiana*, ed. by G. Barbarisi and W. Spaggiari, vol. 3 (Milan: Cisalpino, 2006), pp. 245–6.

social control, the content embedded in the festivals' spectacular frame had to be devised according to the overlapping needs for celebration, solemnization and indoctrination of what has been described as a new 'secular' religion.[157] Arguably the main cultural product of the Revolution, festivals also had to be gradually exported to all lands 'liberated' by the revolutionary armies, fulfilling the mission that France had taken upon itself as the main actor in the process of societal regeneration: part cultural, part political, the festivals amplified the revolutionaries' enthusiasm for liberating themselves and the rest of world from the shackles of the past.[158]

The *Fête de la Fédération* (Festival of the Federation), organized in Paris on 14 July 1790, provides an ideal example of the application of these principles. This festival was organized on a scale described as almost 'mythical' because of its huge symbolic value: as well as the first anniversary of the storming of the Bastille, the attendees celebrated the patriotism shown by the *fédérés* throughout France, the ongoing writing of the Constitution, the covenant with the King and the nationwide *nouvel ordre des choses* that would soon spread to the rest of the world.[159] It also constituted the first large-scale attempt to design a ritual extending beyond existing models, both reframing them and enriching them with new elements.[160] Even though the republic had not yet been proclaimed (France being still a constitutional monarchy), the Festival of the Federation has thus been described as the first true republican feast.[161]

The main celebrations took place in the esplanade stretching from the *École militaire* to the Seine, altered and newly christened as the Champ de Mars. On the day of the festival, the esplanade featured an artificial hill surmounted by an altar dedicated to the nation, a great elliptical amphitheatre, a reconstruction of the Bastille and a colossal *arc de triomphe* (Figure 8).[162] In line with revolutionary aesthetics, these structures (especially the amphitheatre) were designed to visually communicate the importance of the occasion, but also to make sure that the attendees could observe both the ritual and themselves.[163]

---

[157] Ihl, *La fête républicaine*, pp. 39–47.

[158] Hemmings, *Culture and Society in France*, pp. 52–3.

[159] *Confédération Nationale* (Paris: Garnéry, 1790), p. 2. Michelet, *Histoire de la Révolution française*, pp. 8 and 180. Ozouf, *La fête révolutionnaire*, pp. 51–5.

[160] R.-A. Etlin, '*L'architecture et la fête de la fédération*', in *Les fêtes de la Révolution*, conference proceedings, Clermont Ferrand, 24–6 June, ed. by J. Ehrard and P. Viallaneix (Paris: Société des études robespierristes, 1974), pp. 131–2.

[161] C. Bessonnet-Favre, *Les fêtes républicaines depuis 1789 jusqu'à nos jours* (Paris: Gedalge, 1909), pp. 9–11.

[162] *Confédération Nationale*, pp. 119–20.

[163] Mastropasqua, *Le feste della Rivoluzione francese*, pp. 15–16. Etlin, '*L'architecture et la fête de la fédération*', p. 135. Michelet, *Histoire de la Révolution française*, pp. 184–5.

Figure 8 Anonymous, *Plan du Champ de la Confédération* (1790).
© Bibliothèque nationale de France.

This sacralized space, representative of the whole nation, was rich in symbols
of both antiquity and the present, which projected it into a timeless, absolute
dimension and harked back to the glorious 'republican' age of ancient Greece
and Rome.[164] Neoclassical elements, from the altar and tripods to the insignia
carried by the military, were interspersed with pagan and revolutionary symbols
of regeneration such as the Tree of Liberty, Phrygian caps and allegories of
Liberty and the Revolution.[165] The celebrations also included a catholic mass

---

[164] Ozouf, *La fête révolutionnaire*, pp. 58–9. Hunt, *Politics, Culture, and Class in the French
Revolution*, pp. 28–9.

[165] Hemmings, *Culture and Society in France*, p. 54. Etlin, 'L'architecture et la fête de la
fédération', pp. 138–9.

and a Te Deum set to music by a rising star of revolutionary art, François-Joseph Gossec, who scored it for huge choral and instrumental masses, including brass and wind sections reminiscent of military ensembles.[166] With these parallel and overlapping layers of visual and sonic elements, the fête also established the eclectic symbolism – the 'orgy of symbols', as it has been described – which would become a constant of republican festivals.[167]

The celebrations took place following the detailed codification of the new authorities (i.e. the Commune, the National Assembly and the corps of the National Guard). Despite the pouring rain (the 'aristocratic weather', as it was called on the day), the celebrations started with a large-scale procession of the representatives of all social, civic and religious authorities, as well as volunteer militias from all provincial villages and towns.[168] These were followed by representatives of different social groups, from mothers with their babies draped in tricoloured cloths to children carrying insignia inscribed with 'Hope for the Fatherland', while the honour of carrying the civic banner was reserved to each town's oldest citizen. This allegorical representation of the people through its different age groups and social roles was destined to become a major tool of revolutionary pedagogy, and replicated in festivals throughout France and Europe.[169] Replicating a familiar ritual, the procession went through the city's main streets, and entered the Champ de Mars passing under the triumphal arch.

Under the eyes of thousands of spectators, the delegates performed a series of ritual gestures that would inform all future republican celebrations, from the burning of incense on tripods and on the altar to the singing of hymns and the screaming of republican slogans and oaths.[170] A pivotal moment was the oath of fidelity to the nation, the law, the Constitution and the King (who was still seen as the guarantor of the Constitution): prepared by music, cannon fire and 'religious silence', the oath was pronounced first by the commander of the National Guard, Marquis de Lafayette, and this was then followed by the response of all members of the military corps. It was then the turn of the President of the National Assembly, answered by his peers. Finally, the King repeated the formula and was answered by the 15,000 spectators, while the artillery and drums signalled

---

[166] F.-J. Gossec, *Te Deum*, ms score (1790), MS-1430, F-Pn, e.g. pp. 1r and 2r.

[167] Bosisio, '*Un poeta al servizio di un nuovo modello di spettacolo*', p. 247.

[168] See the '*ordre de marche*' in *Confédération Nationale*, pp. 108–10, and Michelet, *Histoire de la Révolution française*, p. 192.

[169] *Rituel républicain* . . . (Paris: Aubry, 1794), p. 1–2. Ozouf, *La fête révolutionnaire*, pp. 64–5. C.-M. Bosséno, '*Le feste civiche*', in *L'Italia nella Rivoluzione, 1789–1799*, exhibition catalogue, Rome, Biblioteca nazionale centrale, 6 March–7 April, ed. by G. Benassati and L. Rossi (Bologna: Grafis, 1990), p. 72.

[170] Mastropasqua, *Le feste della Rivoluzione francese*, pp. 18–19. P. Puppa, '*La coreografia dell'ordine*', *Lo spettacolo nella Rivoluzione francese*, ed. by P. Bosisio (Rome: Bulzoni, 1989), p. 177.

that moment to the whole of Paris; ideally, drummers and soldiers were also stationed in the towns around the capital and further into the province, so that the message would get almost instantly to the four corners of the country.[171] This highly codified use of sonic elements (including the silence in between the 'performances') denotes a particularly refined use of what has been called 'sound-signals', which were able to transmit complex messages (here also amplified by the spectacular setting) to the feast's attendees.[172] The ritualized swearing of the oath and the soundscape of military elements and human voices (also recreated in Gossec's music) rapidly became constants of republican festivals, also in line with the progressive dramatization of the register used for political communication. The power of the ritualized word, traditionally linked to religion and kingship, was soon appropriated by the revolutionaries; the swearing of an oath of fidelity also removed the divine component from the traditional ritual, and rooted all sovereignty in the people assembled, creating a new 'national' consensus.[173] Through occasions such as this, language became an instrument of social and political change, and was already recognized as a paramount instrument of revolutionary propaganda in its early phases.[174] The moment of the swearing of the oath also provided the new/regenerated nation with a foundational moment: the social contract subscribed was repeatedly perpetrated in a constructed 'mythical' present.[175]

Although many chronicles of the time are arguably biased, the feast of 14 July 1790 was a huge success; news quickly reached Paris of thousands of Trees of Liberty being erected in villages and towns across France, accompanied by patriotic music, dances and speeches. This dissemination convinced the authorities that festivals, appositely planned and executed, could provide an effective tool to steer public opinion in the desired direction.[176] The Feast of the Federation can thus be seen as creating an effective cast around which celebrations could be modelled, both in France and in the lands 'liberated' by its armies, to guide society towards its regeneration. As already mentioned, this model repurposed pre-existing elements and juxtaposed them with new ones; while it could be argued that similar processes could be observed in celebrations associated with political change (as in the Milanese 1771 examples), the project

---

[171] *Confédération Nationale*, pp. 134–7. Hemmings, *Culture and Society in France*, p. 55.

[172] Schafer, 'The Soundscape', p. 101. Strohm, *Music in Late Medieval Bruges*, pp. 3–4. Carter, 'The Sound of Silence', pp. 13–14.

[173] Hunt, *Politics, Culture, and Class in the French Revolution*, pp. 20–4.

[174] See, for example, J. F. de La Harpe, *Du fanatisme dans la langue révolutionnaire* ... (Paris: Chaumerot, 1821), pp. 9–11.

[175] Hunt, *Politics, Culture, and Class in the French Revolution*, p. 27. Bithell, 'The Past in Music: Introduction', pp. 4–6.

[176] Hemmings, *Culture and Society in France*, p. 55. Pancera, *'Feste e rituali della rivoluzione'*, pp. 161–2.

underpinning revolutionary festivals can be considered of unparalleled scale, strength and impact. The next section will discuss the features and challenges of the model's implementation in republican Milan, concluding the framework in which the detailed description of the actual events, contained in the following chapter, can be framed.

1.4 The Transplantation: Challenges, Issues and Organisation

The arrival of the French army into Milan was welcomed by semi-spontaneous demonstrations of joy, fuelled by the local 'Jacobins', which took place in the days immediately following the 'triumphal' entry on 15 May. These celebrations, rather small in scale, were organized mainly to show the victorious French that they could count on a strong consensus and to advocate local participation in discussions of freedom and independence;[177] they mostly replicated celebratory codes that had already been long established in Milan, from the lighting of public and private venues to the addition of ad-hoc elements to theatrical performances, but also introduced quintessentially French revolutionary features. On the very evening of Napoleon's entry into Milan, for instance, the French soldiers demanded La Scala to be lit and opened free of charge, and *La Marseillaise* to be performed in between the acts of the scheduled performances (a comedy presented by the Perelli troupe and an opera buffa as part of the spring season) in the presence of Napoleon himself.[178] A few days later (19 May), the recent French victory on the Bridge of Lodi was celebrated with a lavish *festa da ballo* open to everybody, while citizens were requested to light their houses at their own expense.[179] Ironically, that same night the French soldiers robbed Milan's charity fund of enormous quantities of gold, while shortly afterwards the government ordered the city to pay the exorbitant tax of twenty million francs.[180]

Similar demonstrations of joy were offered for the citizens in other French-occupied cities. In Naples, for instance (ruled by yet another of Ferdinand's siblings, the Archduchess Maria Carolina), a carnivalesque performance of *La Marseillaise* was put together in the city's market square on 25 January 1799,

---

[177] Buclon, *Napoléon et Milan*, p. 185.

[178] G. Chiappori, *Serie cronologica delle rappresentazioni drammatico-pantomimiche poste sulle scene dei principali teatri di Milano 1776–1818* (Milan: Silvestri, 1818), p. 53. G. Tintori (ed.), *Duecento anni alla Scala*, exhibition catalogue, Milan, Palazzo Reale, 16 February– 10 September (Milan: Electa, 1978), p. 13. G. Bezzola and G. Tintori, *I protagonisti e l'ambiente della Scala in età neoclassica* (Milan: Il Polifilo, 1984), p. 41.

[179] [Poster] 19 May 1796, I-Mas, AGSP P.A., folder 3. *Giornale storico della Repubblica Cisalpina dall'epoca della sua Libertà e Indipendenza*, ms, vol. 1 (S.Q.+. I. 14), I-Ma, p. 18.

[180] Minola, *Diario storico politico di alcuni avvenimenti del secolo XVIII*, ms, vol. 10 (G 120 suss), I-Ma, p. 30. Cambiasi, *La Scala 1778–1889*, p. 23.

only a couple of days after the arrival of the French troops; the popular tune was set to local tarantellas, and tricoloured flags and ribbons decorated the floats representing the vanquished monarchs.[181]

Milan became not only the capital of a French sister republic but also its main powerhouse to produce propaganda outputs and experiences, and offered an ideal variety of cultural venues and forces; therefore, governmental action was soon devised for the organization of large-scale celebratory events. This took the form of a dedicated *Commissione* especially instituted by the Ministry of Internal Affairs and called many names, including '*per le Pubbliche Feste*' and '*Delegata per le Feste*'. This commission carried out a very intense plan of activities, and had access to almost unlimited funds and labour throughout the republican years. In July 1796, for instance, it organized an evening festival in the public gardens of Porta Orientale (where the *Banchetto delle Spose* had taken place in 1771). For the occasion, the whole area of the gardens was lit *a giorno* (daylight-like) and decorated with tricoloured lamps and ribbons; two pavilions and a temporary theatre were built to accommodate the attendees and host various performances happening simultaneously, from choral, band and orchestral music to spoken theatre.[182] Similarly, a *conto* (invoice) forwarded to the members of the *Commissione* after a four-day festival in spring 1797 shows a long list of items, from the seamstresses who sewed the costumes for the statues of Liberty and Nation to the hundreds of candles lighting the theatres, and from the dozens of instrumentalists and choristers to the carpenters who put together the temporary structures; the *conto* adds up to 4,000 Milanese liras, a significant amount when considering that the average price for a season ticket in La Scala at the time was 100 liras.[183] Large-scale festival-like events such as these seem to have taken place as early as the summer of 1796, and continued until early 1799, when the Austrian army and their Russian allies managed to reconquer Milan and keep it for thirteen months. Once the French came back and a second Cisalpine Republic was established, in 1801, these events immediately resumed, having become an essential feature of political communication.[184]

The utopian atmosphere of spontaneous gathering advocated by the festivals' theorists could be considered lost even before the Napoleonic invasion of Italy, with the authorities carefully controlling every detail of the celebratory ritual. When disseminating its model to the French provinces, the Municipality of Paris transmitted an incredible amount of prescriptive detail: the swearing of the oaths

---

[181] V. Sani, *1799. Napoli. La Rivoluzione* (Venosa, Italy: Osanna, 1799), pp. 75–6. M. Traversier, '*"Transformer la plèbe en peuple". Théâtre et musique à Naples en 1799 …*', in *Annales historiques de la Révolution française* 335 (2004), p. 43.

[182] Criscuolo, *Termometro politico della Lombardia*, vol. 1, pp. 119–122.

[183] [*Conto*], May 1797, I-Mas, AGSP P.A., folder 2.   [184] Buclon, *Napoléon et Milan*, p. 184.

and the speeches, for instance, had to happen at exactly the same time in all corners of the nation, the patriotic toasts had to be pronounced at the same moment at all tables during celebratory banquets and so on. It was a true obsession with unanimity and simultaneity that remained, however, largely confined to utopia; at the provincial level at least, local specificities such as traditional dances or liturgical elements often found their way to the festive frame.[185]

The transplantation of this highly prescriptive model into the Milanese context occasioned a steep increase in the level of planning and control by the French/ republican authorities. Like all other sister republics of France, the Cisalpine Republic received a series of hyper-codified symbols of high pedagogic and propagandistic value, which had long lost any spontaneous character. A notable example is that of the Tree of Liberty, one of the Revolution's most beloved symbols of regeneration, which rapidly became a constant presence in both urban and rural landscapes.[186] Originating as a sober branch or trunk erected during the popular riots in the French countryside, the Tree of Liberty was standardised into a high vertical pole adorned with revolutionary symbols, and crested by a red Phrygian hat: it is this codified model that can be seen in all celebratory images of the Italian republics (see, again, Figure 5). Similar observations can be made regarding the visual elements and rituals embedded in the republican festivals. Already discouraging (when not openly repressing) any spontaneous demonstration of patriotism, festival organizers made sure that all channels of communication were meticulously monitored and all reactions controlled.[187]

Indeed, as Mona Ozouf demonstrated, revolutionary festivals could also be considered a refined form of camouflage concealing the intrusive character of many revolutionary measures, with their highly allegorical/utopian frame embedding a mixture of precautionary and coercive elements.[188] In the case of Milan, where the financial and cultural spoliation was particularly systematic and visible, this camouflage element had to be planned and displayed on a large scale. The engagement of the popular masses (mainly hostile to the concepts of the Revolution and infuriated by the desecration of religious practices) became a structural element of the festivals and was pursued through the offering of entertainment, the constant demonstration of the governors' goodwill and generosity, and the constant invitation to actively listen and participate.[189] While similar channels had already been exploited by the Habsburg governors,

---

[185] Ozouf, *La fête révolutionnaire*, pp. 62–4.   [186] Salvi, *Scenari di libertà*, pp. 120–3.

[187] Bosisio, '*Un poeta al servizio di un nuovo modello di spettacolo*', pp. 246–7. A. Carlini, '*Lo strepitoso risonar de'stromenti da fiato & timballierie . . .*', in *L'aere è fosco, il ciel s'imbruna . . .*, ed. by F. Passadore and F. Rossi (Venice: Edizioni Fondazione Levi, 2000), p. 473.

[188] Ozouf, *La fête révolutionnaire*, pp. 36–7.

[189] Carter, 'Listening to Music in Early Modern Italy', pp. 25–6.

republican festivals would use them more systematically.[190] A notable example
is a festival organized in late 1797 to celebrate the most recent victories of the
French army, which saw solemn celebrations, the distribution of bread, meat
and rice in the parish churches and prisons, and a colossal firework display
mounted on a temporary *arc de triomphe*.[191]

The press, experiencing an increase like no other in the history of Milan, added
yet another layer of controlled communication, also participating in the process of
actively moulding public opinion.[192] Periodicals, especially Salfi's *Termometro
politico* and the *Giornale degli Amici della Libertà e dell'Uguaglianza*, as well as
the numerous government-financed pamphlets, constantly reminded their readers
of the generosity of their new governors, the happiness and freedom they brought,
and the huge success of celebratory events.[193] In striking contrast with previous
years, these publications targeted a wide audience and were characterized by
a rather artificial enthusiasm that soon degenerated into servility. Their editors and
contributors, often lacking any literary background, made use of grandiloquent
oratory, coarse language and theatrical tools, replicating many features of the
rhetoric used in the festivals, and were (privately) ridiculed by intellectuals and
professional writers such as Vittorio Alfieri and Ugo Foscolo.[194] At the same
time, written media were subjected to the same stringent controls as the patriotic
clubs, so that any initiative crossing the borders of prescribed enthusiasm was
harshly repressed. Between October and November 1796, for instance, both the
Termometro politico and the *Giornale degli amici della libertà* were suspended,
with many contributors being arrested for having suggested (as the *clubbisti* had
done in the streets) that Lombardy should gain full independence.[195] Similarly, in
1797, the intellectual and member of the first Cisalpine Municipality Pietro
Custodi denounced in his newspaper *Il Tribuno del popolo* that the Treaty of
Campoformio had betrayed the principles of democracy; he was arrested and
confined to a mental hospital for several years before being reinstated for his
merits as an economist.[196]

---

[190] Bosséno, '*Le feste civiche*', p. 69.

[191] *Descrizione delle feste date in Milano a' 28 e 29 piovoso* ... (Milan: n.n., 1797), p. 5.

[192] Tognarini, '*Le repubbliche giacobine*', p. 71. Fava, *Storia di Milano*, p. 13. Tocchini, '*Dall'antico regime alla Cisalpina*', pp. 44–5.

[193] See, for example, '*Disposizione del popolo milanese a rigenerarsi*' and '*Dialogo tra un milanese e l'Arciduca*', in Criscuolo, *Termometro politico della Lombardia*, vol. 1 (25 June 1796), pp. 86–90, and (28 June 1796), pp. 99–100, respectively. *L'Arciduca Ferdinando spettatore incognito alla gran festa federativa* ... (Milan: n.n., 1797). *Storia della fondazione del Lazzaretto fuori di Porta Orientale* ... (Milan: n.n., 1797).

[194] Cazzamini Mussi, *Il giornalismo a Milano dalle origini alla prima guerra di indipendenza*, p. 110.

[195] 'Introduzione', in Criscuolo, *Termometro politico della Lombardia*, vol. 1, pp. 9–10.

[196] Ottolini, '*La vita culturale nel periodo napoleonico*', p. 409.

To what extent the press mirrored actual public opinion is impossible to determine, but many scholars argue that most Milanese did not agree either with the tireless celebration of the French dominators or with the degree of violence and coarseness used in its articulation.[197] The attendance at republican festivals is a particularly interesting example to consider, as all government-controlled publications seem to perpetuate the image of huge crowds filled with patriotic zeal. With the systematic use of hyperbole and other rhetorical tools, the crowds attending the festivals and other republican celebrations were described with adjectives such as *immenso* (immense) and *enorme* (enormous), and using images such as *inondava le strade* (flooded the streets). Similarly, their enthusiasm and willingness to perform revolutionary gestures (e.g. wearing the tricoloured ribbon, singing and dancing around the Tree of Liberty) are described as overwhelmingly strong throughout.[198] In truth, while the offerings of food and entertainment surely attracted many, and while civic and military authorities had to commit to the ritualized celebration of the revolutionary creed as they traditionally did with religious and civic rituals, many symbols, concepts and gestures embedded in these celebrations remained rather alien. This almost obsessive auto-celebration appeared suspicious even at the time: the anonymous compiler of the *Giornale storico della Repubblica Cisalpina* and an avid (albeit biased) observer of social and cultural life, for instance, commented how:

> ... the word '*libertà*' [freedom] keeps being repeated, as if rulers were scared that the People did not realize they have it ...: this is the reason behind all those long speeches, ... books and newspapers, notes and posters, which proclaim that word until it becomes annoying. A casual observer could notice that this behaviour is typical of those who talk about something they do not really believe in, for whoever is really convinced of something, talks about it fervently, but rarely.[199]

The control of every aspect of events organized in the public space, of associations and of the press, together with the censorship of theatrical and musical performances in specific venues, meant that almost all of the cultural and entertainment experiences that the Milanese had access to were planned by the governing authorities. The following chapter will dive deeper into the features of the *pubbliche feste*, addressing particularly the relationship between

---

[197] Cazzamini Mussi, *Il giornalismo a Milano dalle origini alla prima guerra di indipendenza*, pp. 128–9. De Castro, *Milano e la Repubblica Cisalpina giusta le poesie, le caricature ...*, pp. 93–4.

[198] See, for example, Criscuolo, *Termometro politico della Lombardia*, vol. 1, pp. 119–120, 150, 294 and 340–1.

[199] *Giornale storico della Repubblica Cisalpina dall'epoca della sua Libertà e Indipendenza*, ms, vol. 1 (S.Q. +. I. 14), I-Ma, pp. 70–1.

these events and the urban landscape and soundscape, as well as their consequences for issues of identity and self-representation.

2 The Festivals and the City

2.1 A New Time: The Republican Calendar and Feasts

Following the rich historical, cultural and aesthetical context illustrated in the
previous chapter, it is now time to turn to the main features of the festivals and
other tools of public celebration implemented in Milan during the first republican triennium (1796–9) and the second Cisalpine Republic (1800–2). It will
be beneficial to start the analysis of this systematic intervention by looking at
how the republican government appropriated the two main features shaping
urban/civic life, namely time and space.[200] As in many other coeval cities,
numerous aspects of urban and cultural life in Milan were extensively shaped
by the religious calendar;[201] the organization of the opera house's repertoire
into seasons offering specific types of works (e.g. opera seria during the
carnival season and combinations of comedies and opera buffa during the
spring season), for instance, followed both the Ambrosian calendar and
the sociable needs of the aristocracy, who spent the warmer months in their
pleasure villas in the countryside.[202] All entertainment and performances,
both public and private, were also prohibited during Lent, from the Saturday
after Ash Wednesday to Easter, when religious celebrations worked in concert
with the reopening of the theatre in signalling a rebirth of cultural and social
life.[203] Throughout the eighteenth century, we can also observe a process of
rationalization of urban culture, which made many festive elements leave the
public space and enter the less visible and more regulated space of the codified
venue: this was the case, for instance, with the masked feasts taking place in
the opera house during the carnival season, which increased in both number
and regulation.[204]

During the Habsburg rule, the Ambrosian calendar was juxtaposed with
dynastic events such as royal births, betrothals and visits, which sparked
additional celebrations and cultural outputs, from dedicated theatrical

---

[200] T. Carter, 'Listening to Music in Early Modern Italy', pp. 32–3. Carreras, 'Topography, Sound
and Music', pp. 90–1.

[201] See, for example, Strohm, *Music in Late Medieval Bruges*, p. 3.

[202] Mozzarelli, '*La Villa, la corte e Milano capitale*', pp. 17–18. Hansell, *Opera and Ballet at the
Regio Ducal Teatro of Milan, 1771–1776 . . .*, p. 194.

[203] Valery, *Historical, Literary, and Artistical Travels in Italy*, p. 65.

[204] See the numerous [Documents] in I-Mc, FS, folder 1, and in I-Mas, AGSP P.A., folders 1 and 5.
See also C. Bernardi and C. Bini, '*Ragionevoli culti . . .*', in *La cultura della rappresentazione
nella Milano del Settecento*, ed. by R. Carpani, A. Cascetta and D. Zardin (Rome: Bulzoni,
2010), pp. 458–60.

productions to complex celebrations such as those of 1771.[205] Similarly, deaths or other sad events occasioned significant interruptions in the city's cultural life, with dedicated solemnities in public venues. A notable example was the death of Maria Theresia (1780), when theatres were closed and an elaborate stone catafalque was erected by Piermarini in San Fedele (the seat of the Imperial Chapel after the demolition of Santa Maria alla Scala) to catalyse public mourning and pay homage.[206] Religious and civic calendars, as well as urban traditions and dynastic events, were thus regulating public time, celebration and entertainment on a plurality of levels.

Because of its influence on public habits, time management had been recognized as a powerful tool of control and re-education by revolutionary theorists since 1789, when the idea first arose of 'revolutionising time' by recentring the year around the Storming of the Bastille. The idea of a republican calendar addressed several needs at the heart of the advocated project of regeneration, especially those of rationalizing the religious calendar (e.g. its movable feasts and overabundance of saints days) and of marking the discontinuity with the past and the 'new beginning' of history.[207] The Milanese republican government took immediate action to secure control of the city's time: just a few days after the French army's arrival, the new republican calendar, which had already been in use in France since 1793, was introduced and started to appear consistently in outputs such as proclamations, administrative documents, newspapers and opera librettos.[208] The republican calendar adopted a set of new civic and pagan references, setting 22 September as the first day of the year and 1792 as Year I. In doing so, it centred time perception on both a revolutionary occasion and a highly symbolic, immemorial one (the autumn equinox being the day of perfect 'equality' between day and night).[209] It also introduced twelve 30-day months named after seasonal elements, choosing a system of references to nature rather than any religious or tradition-enshrined structure.[210] After the proclamation of the Cisalpine Republic (April 1797), the French republican

[205] See, for example, A. Salvi, *La Germania trionfante in Arminio* (Milan: G. P. Malatesta, 1739), I-Bc, pp. 3–6, and G. Riviera, *La Gara dei geni nel felice nascimento del Serenissimo arciduca d'Austria Pietro Leopoldo* (Milan: G. P. Malatesta, 1747), I-Mb.

[206] Chiappori, *Serie cronologica delle rappresentazioni drammatico-pantomimiche poste sulle scene dei principali teatri di Milano 1776–1818*, p. 118. Barbieri, Carpani and Mignatti, *Festa, rito e teatro nella gran città di Milano*, pp. 1080–2.

[207] F. Furet and M. Ozouf, *Dictionnaire critique de la Révolution française*, vol. 3, 2nd ed. (Paris: Flammarion, 2007), pp. 91–5. Ozouf, *La fête révolutionnaire*, pp. 188–9.

[208] Moiraghi, *Napoleone a Milano*, p. 58. *Annali della Fabbrica del Duomo di Milano dall'origine fino al presente*, p. 237. G. Palomba, *L'astuta in amore* (Milan: G. B. Bianchi, 1796), I-Mb, p. 2.

[209] Furet and Ozouf, *Dictionnaire critique de la Révolution française*, p. 96.

[210] R. Paulson, *Images of the Revolution (1789–1820)* (New Haven, CT: Yale University Press, 1983), p. 16. P. R. Hanson, *Historical Dictionary of the French Revolution* (Lanham, MD: The Scarecrow Press, 2004), p. 278.

calendar was also juxtaposed with the local one, although the latter was used inconsistently throughout.[211]

Altering the organization and perception of time, which had remained untouched for centuries, had already been a very difficult process in France and was often hindered by scarce popular participation and even by full protests; in 1796 (Year IV), for instance, reports coming from the French provinces still lamented how people 'detested' the new 'national holidays' and did not honour them like religious celebrations on Sundays.[212] In Lombardy/the Cisalpine Republic, the republican calendar constituted yet another imposition that was proudly shown on official documents and outputs, but arguably was not understood or accepted by the popular masses, especially in the countryside.

The main reason behind the alteration to the calendar was, as already mentioned, controlling holidays and other occasions for public celebration and engagement; the implementation of the calendar and that of the festivals cannot be separated.[213] Together with the calendar, the republican government aimed at introducing a whole new system of public feasts, effectively combining time management with propaganda strategies. The new calendar also set a new beginning of time, and gave a *point fixe* against which all later events had to be measured, ultimately altering history: in this sense, it is not a coincidence that the first large-scale and fully staged festival organized in Milan took place on 22 September 1796, which was not only the (fourth) anniversary of the proclamation of the French Republic but also the beginning of the first year under the new calendar.[214] Even the proclamations announcing the upcoming event proudly defined it as Milan's first *festa veramente repubblicana* (truly republican feast), using a rhetoric very similar to that of the 1790 Feast of the Federation.[215]

The festival took the form of a foundation ritual, further solemnized by the presence of Napoleon himself. Following a codified ritual, it started with a procession of the French and Milanese troops and civic authorities marching to the cathedral square, which had been transformed into a grand amphitheatre thanks to the construction of tiered benches and decorated with a colossal statue of Liberty. The ritual saw the Tree of Liberty being planted on an altar dedicated to the Lombard liberation, patriotic speeches, solemn oaths and music provided by two large choral and instrumental ensembles, military instruments and gunfire. The rest of the day until late at night was occupied by events replicating

---

[211] *Giornale storico della Repubblica Cisalpina dall'epoca della sua Libertà e Indipendenza*, ms, vol. 1 (S.Q+I.14), I-Ma, p. 17.

[212] Furet and Ozouf, *Dictionnaire critique de la Révolution française*, p. 102.

[213] Ozouf, *La fête révolutionnaire*, p. 193. Pancera, '*Feste e rituali della rivoluzione*', p. 161.

[214] Buclon, *Napoléon et Milan*, pp. 194–5.

[215] [Posters], 21 September 1797, I-Mas, AGSP P.A., folder 2. *Raccolta degli ordini ed avvisi ...*, vol. 1 (Milan: Veladini, 1796), p. 254.

familiar traditions and targeting the different social classes, including a *pranzo patriottico* and *festa da ballo* for the military and civic authorities in the Palazzo Ducale, the performance of Vittorio Alfieri's tragedy *Virginia* free of charge at the Cannobiana and horse and foot races organized on the castle esplanade.[216] This multilayered celebration, juxtaposing familiar and new elements, constituted, indeed, Milan's first republican festival, marking the beginning of the 'new time' and the assimilation of Milan into the 'immobile history' advocated by the Revolution.[217] The festival took the name *Festa della Federazione* and was celebrated in the local Lazzaretto (leper hospital esplanade) rechristened *Campo di Marte*, with a ritual and setting that almost perfectly recreated that of 1790 in Paris.[218] Interestingly, the next event that matched, or even surpassed, in scale that of September 1796 was the festival celebrated the following year, in July 1797, to mark the foundation of the Cisalpine Republic, with its own calendar, history, heroes and recurrences.

According to the new calendar, the occasions to be celebrated, programmatically replacing religious festivities and carefully spread out throughout the year, were related to events and figures of both the French Revolution and the Italian campaign, with the Cisalpine anniversaries also featuring after 1797. Among these were, for instance, the first day of the republican year (1 Vendémiaire/ 22 September), the execution of Queen Marie Antoinette (25 Vendémiaire/ 16 October), the coup of 18 Brumaire (9 November), the execution of King Louis XVI (2 Pluviôse/21 January) and the Storming of the Bastille (14 July), as well as the victories that the *Armée d'Italie* kept winning in the period 1796–7 while advancing through Lombardy and Veneto. These new feasts were widely advertised through posters, proclamations and public speeches, with their link to the Lombard and Cisalpine people being almost over-explained.[219] At the same time, pamphlets in the format of the popular *decadari* and *almanacchi* (calendars containing information about holidays, feasts and notable events) were published throughout the republican years in all of the Italian cities occupied by the French.[220] A particularly rich example is that of the *Nuovo Decadario per l'anno VI della Repubblica Francese ...* (*New Ten-Month Calendar for the Year VI of the French Republic ...*), published in 1798, which graphically juxtaposed the main dates of the Gregorian calendar with religious holidays,

---

[216] Criscuolo, *Termometro politico della Lombardia*, vol. 1, pp. 339–42 (24 September 1796).

[217] Bosséno, '*Le feste civiche*', p. 70.

[218] *L'Arciduca Ferdinando spettatore incognito alla gran festa federativa*, pp. 6–16.

[219] [Printed speeches], 1797–1801, I-Mas, AGSP P.A., folders 1 and 2. Moiraghi, *Napoleone a Milano*, p. 20.

[220] See, for example, *Almanacco italiano e francese per l'anno 1796 ...* (Milan: F. Bolzani, 1796); *Della instruzione nazionale ...* (Cremona, Italy: Feraboli, 1799); *I fasti repubblicani ...* (Milan: Pirola, 1802); *Tavole di ragguaglio pel confronto delle date ...* (Milan: Borsani, 1805).

Figure 9 Excerpt from *Nuovo decadario per l'anno VI della Repubblica francese . . .* (1798).

© Biblioteca civica di Monza.

saints days and events related to the ongoing Italian campaign (Figure 9).[221] These publications allowed the republican government to appropriate a format traditionally associated with religion in order to illustrate the new festivities to the lower social strata and rural masses, also feeding into the ongoing processes of de-Christianisation and rationalization.[222] Many other outputs (e.g. pamphlets, theatre pieces and journal articles) in fact contained a reinterpretation of religious elements based on republican propaganda, from catechisms and prayers such as *Pater noster* and *Credo*, to figures such as priests and nuns.[223]

---

[221] *Nuovo decadario per l'anno VI della Repubblica francese* (Milan: Orena Malatesta, 1798), p. 13.

[222] L. De Salvo and A. Sindoni (eds.), *Tempo sacro e tempo profano* (Soveria Mannelli, Italy: Rubbettino, 2002), pp. 233–4.

[223] See, for example, De Castro, *Milano e la Repubblica Cisalpina giusta le poesie, le caricature . . .*, pp. 129–30, and the series 'Il parroco repubblicano' ('The republican vicar') in Criscuolo, *Termometro politico della Lombardia*, vol. 1, pp. 129–30 (12 July 1796) and 160–1 (26 July 1796).

These measures were complemented by the ongoing sacralization of new elements (e.g. nature and the martyrs of liberty in ancient Rome and Greece) that were ubiquitous in both public festivals and theatrical performances.[224] The intrusive character of these initiatives was highlighted by eyewitnesses, for instance by the compiler of the *Giornale storico della Repubblica Cisalpina*, who called the 1797 *Nuovo decadario* 'a fraud ... to tell us how we are forced to squander our hours and days'.[225] Interestingly, the republican calendar did not have an impact on the structuring of operatic seasons, which continued to follow the traditional labels and periodization: a stronger intervention in terms of subject matter and theatrical practices (discussed in the next chapter) had to be devised. The new calendar did, however, deeply change both time perception and public celebration, adding another layer of theatralization to the setting of republican festivals. This worked particularly well in conjunction with the systematic alteration of public landscape and soundscape, which will be discussed in the next sections.

2.2 A New Space: Destroying and Rechristening

The control of the public space and of its associations through a process of destruction and recreation can be considered one of the most prominent measures implemented by republican regimes both in France and in its sister republics. The ideas of 'purging' spaces of their traditional associations with the *Ancien-Régime* and of filling the void with an array of carefully planned symbols were perfectly in line with the overarching idea of regeneration. Scholars of the French Revolution have explored the concept of 'revolutionary vandalism' at length, recognizing its duplicity between a systematic (albeit not always rational) process with a clear aesthetics and justification on the one hand, and an irrational, unregulated impulse on the other.[226] Different phases of the Revolution also saw different relationships with the visual heritage of the past, in line with its chaotic narrative; a defining feature of revolutionary iconoclasm is, however, that, on a much wider scale than earlier examples, it seems to be motivated by a violent sentiment of revenge on the past, supremely consummated in the destruction of material heritage. As François Souchal has noted, the fervour and enthusiasm of the revolutionary iconoclasts appears very similar to religious fanaticism, further reinforcing

---

[224] Ozouf, *La fête révolutionnaire*, p. 191. Paulson, *Images of the Revolution (1789–1820)*, p. 17.

[225] *Giornale storico della Repubblica Cisalpina dall'epoca della sua Libertà e Indipendenza*, ms, vol. 2 (S.Q+I.15), I-Ma, pp. 4r and 28.

[226] See, for example, F. Souchal, *Le vandalisme de la Révolution* (Paris: Novelles Éditions Latines, 1993), pp. 17–18. Paulson, *Images of the Revolution (1789–1820)*, pp. 3–4.

the proximity between desecration/re-sacralization and revolutionary regeneration.[227] Similarly, Hannah Arendt has identified the association between destructive behaviour and the ideal establishment of the 'new' and the 'altogether-different' as one of the defining features of revolution, and working very well with the underlying 'explosion' of political activism.[228]

Like many other cities occupied by the French, Milan was inserted into the process of destruction and regeneration advocated by the Revolution and, as such, saw copious examples of both vandalism and recreation. With the value that revolutionary theorists placed on language and words (especially highly symbolic ones), one of the most visible measures implemented was that of rechristening public spaces. This had antecedents in Paris, where streets, squares and buildings had been rechristened with names coming from newly sacralized objects/spheres (e.g. nature, heroes from antiquity and concepts associated with the new political creed; *Place Louis XVI*, for instance (close to the Champ de Mars) was rechristened *Place de la Révolution* in 1790.[229] Similarly, in 1793, the National Assembly had approved a 'nonsensical' proposition to transform various cathedrals and churches – the religious and symbolic (as well as topographical) centres of towns and cities – into temples dedicated to the *Raison*.[230] In Paris, *Temple de la Raison* was even chiselled on the façade of Notre Dame, while numerous paintings, crests and sculptures were covered, altered or destroyed. Notre Dame's passage from Christian to revolutionary shrine was also marked by a large-scale pageant, where actresses representing Liberty and Reason took possession of the temple as its new divinities.[231] The rechristening of public spaces, deeply altering their perception and use, thus came to be important foundation rituals, often placed at the core of large-scale celebrations.

In Milan, the preambles of the republican triennium (especially the period between Napoleon's entry in May 1796 and the end of the summer) were characterized by episodes of violent vandalism, almost advocating a total erasure of the past. Mirroring the extreme measures debated in the political clubs, these episodes mainly targeted the symbols of the traditional institutions, now recognized as tyrannical and obsolete (i.e. the Church and the monarchical government (both Habsburg and Spanish)). The sacred images traditionally positioned at street junctions, for instance, were shattered or covered with plaster overnight

---

[227] Souchal, *Le vandalisme de la Révolution*, pp. 27–8.

[228] H. Arendt, *On Revolution* (New York: Viking Press, 1963), pp. 28–9.

[229] Mastropasqua, *Le feste della Rivoluzione francese*, p. 15.

[230] H. Engrand, *Leçons élémentaires sur l'Histoire de France* ... (Reims : Le Batard, 1816), pp. 240–2. C. Cerf and P. C. Hannesse, *Histoire et description de Notre-Dame* ... (Reims: P. Dubois, 1861), pp. 248–50.

[231] Paulson, *Images of the Revolution (1789–1820)*, pp. 16–17.

by a commission of public officers, torchbearers and workmen, although the common people – eyewitnesses reported – kept crossing themselves and taking their hats off.[232] Similarly, after the municipality promulgated a decree to abolish all titles and peerages, all visible symbols representing either the aristocratic or the clerical enemies were hitherto banished. All crests, coat of arms and symbols of nobility and royalty were chiselled off catafalques, portals, graves and buildings;[233] a police committee was even created to survey the Duomo (like Notre Dame, the religious and topographic centre of the city) in order to identify all visual elements to be altered or destroyed, including gravestones to be flipped over so that the dedications could not be read anymore.[234] The production of new images also had to be controlled: for instance, the municipality ordered the *Fabbrica del Duomo* (the institution presiding over the building, refurbishing and decoration of the cathedral) to commission no paintings or statues without governmental approval.[235] The destruction of titles and symbols was also portrayed, often with a satirical twist, in coeval iconography, for instance in caricatures and propagandistic engravings (an example is shown in Figure 10).

Traditional behaviours and practices were also targeted, which, in conjunction with the ongoing process of iconoclasm, greatly altered both the urban landscape and the daily lives of many. Glad tidings such as military victories, for instance, triggered semi-spontaneous actions that disturbed or impeded traditional civic and societal life.[236] In April 1797, for instance, the ongoing congress of Leoben and the prospect of a 'free and independent' Cisalpine Republic triggered a gathering of patriots (the city's 'vilest scum' according to the compiler of the *Giornale storico*), who traversed the city screaming and playing military drums, and forced whoever they met to abandon their work and join them.[237] Some vernacular verses also paint a vivid picture of the changes brought by the ongoing process of eradication of the past to the religious practices regulating the life of many Milanese:

> It was forbidden to bring communion to the sick,
> To bring the statues in procession . . .,
> To worship the Saints,
> To ring the bells,

---

[232] De Castro, *Milano e la Repubblica Cisalpina giusta le poesie, le caricature* . . ., pp. 89–90.

[233] Salvi, *Scenari di libertà*, pp. 126–8.

[234] Fava, *Storia di Milano*, p. 16. *Annali della Fabbrica del Duomo di Milano dall'origine fino al presente*, pp. 242–3.

[235] *Annali della Fabbrica del Duomo di Milano dall'origine fino al presente*, p. 240.

[236] De Castro, *Milano e la Repubblica Cisalpina giusta le poesie, le caricature* . . ., p. 126.

[237] *Giornale storico della Repubblica Cisalpina dall'epoca della sua Libertà e Indipendenza*, ms, vol. 1 (S.Q+I.14), I-Ma, p. 15.

Figure 10 1796 anonymous engraving entitled 'Eguaglianza'.
© Civica Raccolta delle Stampe
'Achille Bertarelli', Castello Sforzesco, Milan.

> To administer the rites on holidays,
> To take the dead to the cemetery,
> To give moral guidance to the young.[238]

Vandalism, iconoclasm and the disruption of traditional symbols and practices, in line with their role in the Revolution's framework, were accompanied by measures aimed at filling the voids or grey areas created with new, carefully planned elements. The practice of rechristening public spaces, often within a lavish celebration, was systematically adopted, while the construction of temporary or semi-permanent structures can be considered, in striking opposition to Habsburg policies, the most significant measure implemented by the republican government in terms of urban planning.[239] A particularly notable example is that of the vast

---

[238] Fumagalli, *L' ultima messa celebrata nella chiesa della Rosa in Milano* ..., p. 11.
[239] Robuschi, *Milano*, pp. 123–4.

Figure 11 D. Aspari, 'Festa della federazione della repubblica cisalpina . . .' (1797). © Bibliothèque nationale de France.

esplanade that surrounded the *Lazzaretto* or leper hospital, previously used during epidemics as a 'safe space' separating the sick from the healthy, and chosen as the location for the already mentioned *Festa federativa* of the Cisalpine Republic in July 1797. As the chosen foundation site of the new republic, the space underwent a process of highly symbolic decoration (Figure 11), which mirrored the Parisian model very closely while inputting some 'local' features.

A triumphal arch was erected at the esplanade's entrance, ready to welcome the procession of military and civic authorities and the immense crowd: the arch was covered with symbols deemed 'appropriate for the celebration' and flanked by two statues of Liberty and Equality. Inside the elliptical space stood a religious and a secular altar destined to be used by both the archbishop and civic authorities.[240] The hospital chapel had also been transformed into a temple of Liberty adorned with obelisks, medals and Etruscan vases, celebrating both the heroes of antiquity and the martyrs of the recent Italian campaign.[241] Tiered benches for spectators were also provided, while flags, weapons and military instruments completed the picture. The foundation ritual of the Cisalpine Republic included a religious liturgy with the archbishop blessing the tricoloured flags, as well as a secular one involving the lighting of a sacred fire,

---

[240] *Dettaglio, e spiegazione della festa federativa celebrata in Milano* ... (Milan: Pulini al Bocchetto, 1797), pp. 4–5.

[241] *L'Arciduca Ferdinando spettatore incognito alla gran festa federativa*, pp. 2–3.

a patriotic speech and the solemn oath of fidelity. Removed from its daily function and becoming a sacred space through the modification of pre-existing structures and the erections of new ones, the esplanade was rechristened *Campo delle Federazione* or *Campo di Marte*.

Another notable example of rechristening through the modification and recreation of the public space is that of the festival celebrated just under four years later, in April 1801, to solemnize the birth of the second Cisalpine Republic after the Austrian interregnum of 1799–1800 and the victory of Marengo. Given the importance of the occasion (the ensuing Treaty of Lunéville officializing the French control over Northern Italy), Milan's amplest esplanade was chosen i.e. *Piazza Castello* (Castle Square). The space hosted the *Castello sforzesco* (Sforza Castle), a symbol of the *Ancien Régime* but also of the glorious epochs of the Sforza and Lombard League.[242] The castle was also the city's main stronghold and often the setting of military parades and evolutions (an example is shown in Figure 12), thus offering the perfect location for the repurposing or destruction of existing associations, as well as for the glorification of Napoleon and his army that had made the rebirth of the republic

Figure 12 D. Aspari, 'Veduta del R.I. Castello di Milano . . .' (1790).
© The British Library Board, Cartographic Items Maps 7.TAB.12.

---

242 Robuschi, *Milano*, p. 123.

possible. The elaborate modification of the space included the demolition of parts of the fortress (some of which even took place during the actual festival, for enhanced drama) and the construction of temporary structures of unparalleled scale.[243] Among these, attendees could see a monument imitating Trajan's Column, decorated with bas-reliefs depicting the events of the latest military campaigns and crested with a colossal statue of Peace, a circular temple dedicated to Immortality, an amphitheatre and an altar consecrated to the fallen soldiers (Figure 13).[244]

The architect Giovanni Antolini had even been commissioned to contribute to the ambitious project of an ancient-Rome-inspired forum with fourteen permanent buildings, surrounded by a colossal colonnade; due to the costs of the ongoing military campaign and the scale of the project, Antolini's *Foro* was never completed.[245] In 1801, the project was, however, very much still alive: during the festival, the new forum's foundation stone was laid, and the

Figure 13 Anonymous, 'Paix célébrée à Milan dans le Forum Bonaparte, le 10 floréal an IX'.

© Bibliothèque nationale de France.

---

[243] A. Palidda, '*D'un bel canto patrioto francese* ...', in *Journal of War & Culture Studies* 14/2 (2021), pp. 179–80.

[244] *Programma della festa per la celebrazione della pace* (Milan: n.n., 1801), I-Mb, Misc. KK. IV.10, pp. 2–4.

[245] Robuschi, *Milano*, pp. 124–5.

esplanade was officially consecrated as *Foro Bonaparte* (a name that the area still retains). This name effectively juxtaposed the homage to antiquity and that to Napoleon, furthering the process of utopian appropriation of the past, as well as of public time and space.[246] The direct reference to Napoleon can be also seen as articulating the ongoing mutation of his role, from military hero to First Consul (after the coup of Brumaire in November 1799), soon-to-become Emperor of the French (1804) and King of Italy (1805); the tools of political communication and engagement and the overarching aesthetical frame can be considered, however, those of 'traditional' republican festivals.

In addition to these particularly spectacular celebrations, Milan also saw many smaller-scale events that modified many popular spaces in its urban landscape. The most notable example is arguably that of the *Porte* or gates, located on the city's outer walls at the junctions with the main roads, and playing a very important role in the city's geography by linking it with the outside. Entering through a specific *Porta* had long been a choice pondered by royals and clerks, as each gate also carried geographical and cultural associations. Archbishops and other religious authorities, for instance, were traditionally received through *Porta Ticinese* (the south-west gate pointing towards Pavia); monarchs, by contrast, used *Porta Romana* (the south-east gate pointing towards Rome).[247] Archduke Ferdinand's wedding procession had already introduced a visible change by entering Milan through *Porta Orientale*, the north-eastern gate pointing towards Vienna, strengthening the ideal link between the Lombard and Habsburg capitals.[248] Finally, Napoleon's entry in 1796 was through *Porta Romana* because of its proximity to Lodi, where the *Armée d'Italie* had won its decisive victory. Throughout the republican years, the main city gates were renamed and sometimes even visually altered: in June 1801, for instance, *Porta Ticinese* was rebuilt *in miglior forma* (in better form) and renamed *Porta Marengo* to celebrate the battle of the same name (1800).[249] After his victory at Marengo, Napoleon in fact made his entry into Milan (this time a truly triumphal one after the repressive Austrian interregnum) through that gate.[250] *Corso di Porta Ticinese* overflowed with songs, applause and tricoloured ribbons; that same evening, a solemn Te Deum was sung in the Duomo in the presence of Napoleon himself, who, as it was customary for monarchs, entered the

---

[246] Bithell, 'The Past in Music', pp. 7–8.   [247] D'Amia, '*La città fatta teatro*', pp. 101–3.

[248] Bertarelli and Monti, *Tre secoli di vita milanese*, pp. 217–18.

[249] [Programma], 25 Prairial Year IX/14 June 1801, I-Mas, AGSP P.A., folder 2, *Sopra il nome di Porta Marenco* ... (Milan: Pirotta e Maspero, 1809). M. A. Crippa and F. Zanzottero, *Le porte di Milano* (Milan: n.n., 1999), p. 158.

[250] Rota, '*Milano napoleonica*', pp. 124–5. Fava, *Storia di Milano*, p. 24.

Figure 14 L. Canonica and A. Sanquirico, 'Entrata di Napoleone in Milano da Porta Marengo nel 1800' (n.d.).
© Comune di Milano Palazzo Moriggia, Museo del Risorgimento.

cathedral under a celebratory baldachin.[251] The striking difference between this entry and that of 1796 made quite an impression on the authorities, who announced the renaming of the gate and the beginning of its reconstruction process over the course of a lavish feast celebrated in June 1801. This included a general procession; a sacralizing ritual made up of speeches, symbolic gestures and patriotic music; and spectacles such as military evolutions. Ironically, the scale of the works necessary to transform the old medieval gate into the large-scale propylaea designed by architect Luigi Cagnola was too large for the project to be completed even by the Austrian Restoration (1814).[252] Although many celebratory engravings produced during the Kingdom of Italy showed a neoclassical gate already at the time of Napoleon's 1800 entry (an example is shown in Figure 14), the project would only be completed in 1815; despite its rededication to Peace, it would remain known as *Porta Marengo* until well after the Unification (1861).[253]

---

[251] Bertarelli and Monti, *Tre secoli di vita milanese*, p. 470. De Castro, *Milano e la Repubblica Cisalpina giusta le poesie, le caricature . . .*, p. 312.

[252] G. Strafforello, *La Patria. Geografia dell'Italia*, ed. by G. Chiesi, vol. 10 (Turin: UTE, 1894), p. 212.

[253] See, for example, F. Palgrave, *Handbook for Travellers in Northern Italy*, 11th ed. (London: J. Murray, 1869), p. 180.

Other city gates were renamed, although with smaller scale celebrations and expenditure; these included the old *Porta Orientale*, which played an important role in the city's geography in its Habsburg times, pointing not only towards Vienna but also in the direction of Monza and the *Villa reale*.[254] Although the exterior aspect of the *Porta Orientale* was not changed, the gate was renamed *Porta Riconoscenza* (Gratitude Gate), hinting at the sentiment that the Cisalpine/Lombard felt towards the French for liberating them from despotism.[255] Finally, the city's ideal axis was reoriented towards the north-west, in the direction of France: in 1807, Cagnola curated the project for a new gate to be called *Porta Sempione* (Simplon Gate), a tribute to the pass and road connecting France and Italy through the Alps. The gate, shaped like an *arc de triomphe* crested with the allegorical representation of Victory and ideally aligned with its Parisian counterpart (started in 1806), was only completed in 1838, and ironically renamed *Arco della Pace* (Arch of Peace, a name still in use) as a tribute to the stability brought by the Restoration.[256]

Not only city gates but also roads, which were traditionally dedicated to saints, corporations or geographical elements, were renamed after the new pantheon of republican heroes, whose names the majority of inhabitants had never heard, but which rapidly became a constant presence in speeches, decorative elements and theatrical performances.[257] These changes were frequently accompanied by acts of destruction or alteration; a notable example is the case of Philip II of Spain's statue, whose head was replaced with that of Brutus.[258] The intrusive, albeit tragi-comical, character of many of these acts was also targeted by satire: in the case of Brutus' statue, for instance, a pamphlet entitled *La famosa contesa tra il busto e la testa della statua di Bruto . . .* (*The Famous Dispute between the Bust and Head of Brutus' Statue . . .*) put forth the idea that the contrast between republican rhetoric and traditional values was an issue not solely for the statue, but for the majority of the Milanese.[259]

The destruction and/or repurposing of decorative elements on public buildings, institutional and private venues; the often-solemnized rechristening and spectacular alteration of spaces; and the tension towards the change of traditional practices and behaviour can be seen as occasioning a general shift not only in Milan's exterior appearance but also in the city's perception by its inhabitants. The combination of these processes, systematically detailed and

[254] Crippa and Zanzottero, *Le porte di Milano*, p. 42.

[255] *Giornale storico della Repubblica Cisalpina dall'epoca della sua Libertà e Indipendenza*, ms, vol. 1 (S.Q+I.14), I-Ma, pp. 118–21. Moiraghi, *Napoleone a Milano*, p. 58.

[256] G. De Finetti, *Milano. Costruzione di una città*, ed. by G. Cislaghi, M. De Benedetti and P. Marabelli (Milan: Hoepli, 2002), p. 65. Robuschi, *Milano*, p. 125.

[257] Del Bianco, *Il coraggio e la sorte*, p. 59.   [258] Salvi, *Scenari di libertà*, p. 129.

[259] *La famosa contesa tra il busto e la testa della statua di Bruto . . .* (Milan: n.n., 1798), pp. 3–4.

implemented by the government authorities and their urban branches, such as the city police and the *Commissione delle Feste*, placed Milan in the process of historiographical reframing originally advocated by the Revolution. This over-arching purpose was also merged with local specificities such as the forging of a Cisalpine/Italian historiography and the evolution of Milan as Napoleon's Italian capital, both having long-lasting consequences in terms of 'national' identity and cultural production. In this context, the following section will explore yet another layer of intervention and change, that of the soundscape and music of republican Milan.

2.3 Music and Sounds of the Festivals

The Model

Within this highly codified setting, performing arts and especially music played a paramount role within republican celebrations as effective tools for both solemnization and entertainment. As already discussed, the exaltation of con-cepts, events and figures constituted the main purpose of many festivals, a purpose towards which all arts and their expressive means had to be geared. Napoleon himself was particularly aware of the important role that the arts played in the revolutionary frame, as well as in terms of personal propaganda.[260] Revolutionary France provided a well-codified model also with regard to the sonorous aspects of the festivals. In particular, music and sounds were entrusted with a specific pedagogical role, very different from entertainment or pleasure: music to be used in festivals – commented an eyewitness in 1794 – was composed not to make hearts soften but rather to inspire them towards republican actions.[261] Parisian performances and institu-tions had been experimenting with musical repertoires and sonic features since the beginning of the 1790s: repurposing music and sounds towards public engagement and education meant designing new ways of conceiving and using them, most notably mixing different, pre-existing and newly supplied repertoires. Patriotic tunes, for instance, had started to be performed at the beginning and in between the acts of operas, while songs based on celebrated *timbres* (melodies) coming from opera and vaudeville were frequently used in the festivals and other celebrations in the city's public spaces.[262] In parallel, the Parisian festivals, as well as other forms of celebration such as parades and

---

[260] A. Pillepich, *Milan capitale napoléonienne: 1800–1814* (Paris: Lettrage, 2001), p. 407.

[261] *Rituel républicain*, p. ix.

[262] C. Pierre, *Les Hymnes et les chansons de la Révolution* (Paris: Imprimerie nationale, 1904), pp. 9–11. L. Mason, *Singing the French Revolution* ... (Ithaca, NY: Cornell University Press, 1996), pp. 34–5. H. Schneider, 'The Sung Constitutions of 1792 ...' in *Music and the French Revolution*, ed. by M. Boyd (Cambridge: Cambridge University Press, 1992), pp. 249–50.

funerals, had seen the production of ad-hoc music, especially engaging pieces such as grand choral numbers and instrumental works with a military flavour. The abundance of occasions and their highly prescriptive nature had forced many artists to quickly adapt to the new style, performers and commissions.[263] Choral tunes, for instance, had to be engaging and simple, so that they could be learned and sung by largely untrained masses with little or no rehearsal, while large-scale pieces saw military bands and classically trained musicians performing together. Very often, composers were also commissioned to write the pieces with just a few days' notice, and had to put together performances of unseen scope and scale.[264]

Furthermore, existing theatrical repertoires had started to be repurposed around subject matter deemed appropriate for the people's moral education; especially after 1793 (when the *Convention nationale* published a law forcing theatres to put on patriotic works), control over public venues in order to impede any 'non-civic' performances and promote 'appropriate' ones became more stringent.[265] The artists having to supply music for the festival were invited to experiment with the rich palette of musical theatre genres in use in the French capital, from grand opera to divertissement. A representative example is that of Gossec, who, with the poet Marie-Joseph Chenier, in early 1793 produced the one-act divertissement *Le Triomphe de la République* to commemorate the French victory against the Prussians at Valmy (September 1792). In order to focus on the valorous soldiers who had defeated the Prussian enemy, Gossec implemented many features of military music, from instruments such as *fifres* (small flutes) and cannons to forms such as marches and hymns.[266] The performance was also preceded by a *jolie mélodie villageoise* (sweet village-style song) and included a processional scene that recreated very closely the *cortèges* of the festivals.[267] Even though it was performed at the conservative Opéra, the divertissement blurred a number of boundaries between spaces and occasions, on the one hand furthering the dynamics triggered by the festivals and, on the other hand, adding yet another layer of intervention on the operatic stage.

---

[263] See the examples catalogued in C. Pierre, *Musique des fêtes et cérémonies de la Révolution française* (Paris: Imprimerie nationale, 1899).

[264] Hemmings, *Culture and Society in France*, pp. 49–50.

[265] J. B. Duvergier, *Collection complete des lois, decrets, ordonnances . . .*, vol. 6 (Paris: Guyot et Scribe, 1825), p. 85. M. Darlow, *Staging the French Revolution . . .* (Oxford: Oxford University Press, 2012), pp. 151–4.

[266] F.-J. Gossec, *Le Triomphe de la République ou Le Camp de Grand Pré*, libretto by M.-J. Chénier (Paris: Huguet, n.d.), F-Pn, pp. 4, 106–7.

[267] Gossec, *Le Triomphe de la République ou Le Camp de Grand Pré*, p. 25. F. Clément and P. Larousse, *Dictionnaire lyrique . . .* (Paris: Administration du grand dictionnaire universel, 1869), p. 133.

During their ritualized performances within the festivals, many pieces of music were also systematically used in alternation with other sonic items, such as spoken word and non-musical sounds/noises. In the Feast of the Federation in 1790, for instance, the ritualized swearing of the foundation oath had been framed by a carefully planned succession of sonorous moments, namely music *la plus imposante* (particularly impressive) to elevate the attendees' thoughts, cannon fire to signal the beginning of the ceremony to the whole of Paris and a prescribed 'religious' silence to make the oath's words stand out. In addition, 300 drums and military sounds accompanied the ceremony, while Gossec's majestic Te Deum provided the background for the conclusive moment of thanksgiving.[268] These often-unprecedented. juxtapositions occasioned the blurring or breaking of many barriers traditionally separating sound and noise, performers and spectators, continuing the reflection on active participation and on the blending of performance components that characterized the very theorization of festivals.[269]

Especially as part of large-scale festivals, music and sounds were also used in conjunction with visual elements, from individual gestures to mass choreographies, furthering the already mentioned sound-signals into powerful 'auditory images' or 'phono-symbols' that constituted even more powerful tools of popular education.[270] A notable example is that of the *Fête de l'Être supreme* (Feast of the Supreme Being), a grand festival organized in 1794 to address the people's spiritual needs by establishing a new, 'civic' or 'natural' religion based on Reason and popular sovereignty.[271] The festival's abstract frame demanded an almost unprecedented display of tools of engagement and communication, which translated into numerous musical pieces and particularly rich audiovisual rituals. Citizens, for instance, were invited not only to light their houses and streets but also to decorate them with the national colours, while the *cortèges* saw an unparalleled sophistication in terms of grouping, costumes and symbols. The celebrations also saw the actions set out in Table 1, which were systematically 'choreographed' to music/sound.

Musical pieces included instrumental symphonies and marches, patriotic songs/airs and large-scale anthems/hymns either produced by favourites of the

---

[268] *Confédération Nationale . . .*, pp. 135–8.

[269] Ferrone, 'La danse fut suspendue . . .', pp. 28–31. Mastropasqua, *Le feste della Rivoluzione francese*, pp. 18–19. J. Livesey, *Making Democracy in the French Revolution* (Cambridge, MA: Harvard University Press, 2001), pp. 210–12.

[270] Carlini, 'Lo strepitoso risonar de' stromenti da fiato & timballierie . . .', pp. 473–4.

[271] J.-P. Domecq, 'La Fête de l'Être suprême et son interprétation', in *Esprit* 154/9 (1989), pp. 113–15.

Table 1 Visual and sonic choreography at the *Fête de l'Être supreme*

Actions	Sonic accompaniment
Start of the celebrations: *cortège* to the *Champ de la Réunion*	Gunfire and drum rolls
The members of the Convention descend from the pavilion into the amphitheatre	Music from military bands
The president approaches the centre of the amphitheatre and sets fire to a figure representing atheism	Symphony
President's speech	Songs and 'joyful' cries of response
Cortège moving again	Drum rolls
During the *cortège*	Patriotic tunes
	Performance of the *Hymne à la Divinité* by Deschamps/Bruny
Return to the *Champ* and positioning of the various groups	Another hymn dedicated to Divinity and a symphony
Tribute of the various groups to the republic (different gestures for each group)	Strophes sung by each group to the tune of the *Marseillaise* with trumpet fanfares and choral responses
	After the final strophe and refrain: gunfire and cries of *'vive la République!'*[272]

system, such as Gossec, Chénier and Deschamps, or modelled around pre-existing material coming from musical theatre, patriotic songs or folk songs.[273] The juxtaposition of different materials, repertoires and performers, and the systematic use of sonorous and sonic elements within a wider performative/spectacular frame, can be seen as creating a unique soundscape and sensory experience for the attendees/participants. Through occasions such as this, music and sound were turned into a real mass medium, a tool of communication and engagement that was systematically geared towards the engagement of wider and more diversified social strata, and a model to be exported to all 'liberated' lands.

---

[272] *Rituel républicain*, pp. 3–13.
[273] *Rituel républicain*, pp. 28–51 and 57–9. C. Laforte, *Le catalogue de la chanson folklorique française*, vol. 6 (Quebec: La Presse de l'Université Laval, 1983), p. 95. *La clé du caveau* ... (Paris: Capelle et Renand, 1811), p. 65.

The Milanese Experience

With the sonorous dimension becoming a core component of festivals and celebrations, many features of the Parisian model outlined above were transplanted into France's sister republics, including the Cisalpine Republic. Here, French products or models were used alongside pre-existing musical material, occasioning location-specific encounters across a range of occasions and venues. In Milan, this process was particularly significant with regard to musical theatre, which was considered the repertoire/occasion at the highest level of sophistication, visibility and societal prominence. At this point, Milan's operatic scene was still rather conservative in terms of repertoire, not to mention tightly linked to the memory of the Habsburg governors and to the sociable needs and financial investments of the aristocracy.[274] The process of blurring the boundaries between this traditionally conservative sphere, the outside space and a set of new/foreign features is thus particularly interesting, and was rich in long-lasting consequences. While the effects of the new regime on operatic and ballet repertoires performed within La Scala and La Cannobiana theatres will be discussed later on, the present section aims to produce an overview of the different ways in which music and sounds were used within the Milanese public celebrations having a republican matrix.

Both archival documents related to the work of the *Commissione delle Feste* and chronicles of the time show how republican celebratory events organized in Lombardy since the very beginning of the French occupation (May 1796) consistently included a vast array of musical performances, with many occasions including different musical events running in succession or even simultaneously to cater for the celebratory and entertainment needs of different social groups. An overview of how different kinds of musical events could be embedded within a public feast can be seen, for instance, in the articles that Salfi published in his *Termometro politico* on the day following a particular celebration, usually to inform the people of its (wonderful) outcome. Although Salfi was notoriously prone to exaggeration, his reports show the sheer variety and complexity of the music provided and provide interesting details on how musical and sonic elements were used. On 16 Messidor Year IV (4 July 1796), for instance, the *Termometro* reported how 'a triple feast with dance, instrumental and vocal music, together with solemn speeches' had taken place in Lodi's public gardens.[275] Four days later, on 20 Messidor (8 July), a majestic celebration took place in Milan's lavishly lit and decorated gardens, where:

---

[274] Degrada, '*Le esperienze milanesi di Mozart*', pp. 738–9.
[275] Criscuolo, *Termometro politico della Lombardia*, vol. 1, p. 120 (4 July 1796).

> Two great ensembles competed in playing various vocal and instrumental
> pieces . . . . On one side, French [military] bands made republican marches
> resound; on the other side, a choir of male and female voices, among which
> stood out that of [Cecilia] Bolognesi, repeatedly sang that very celebrated
> song about human rights written by a Neapolitan patriot, but set to new,
> energetic music. . . . A free theatre offered the more tranquil patrons the calm
> entertainment of the scene while, at the ground floor of an elaborately-
> decorated lodge, two instrumental ensembles invited the brightest youth to
> dance.[276]

Despite its grandiloquent tone, Salfi's report allows us to formulate a few
relevant observations on how the French model for the use of music within
republican feasts was implemented merely three weeks after the arrival of
Napoleon's army. Firstly, the feast saw the interplay between different performers, some local (e.g. the instrumental ensembles playing dance music and the
choirs) and some French (the military bands). The singer mentioned, Cecilia
Bolognesi, was a soprano who had been active in La Scala since 1791, and the
choristers performing without audience participation were in all probability also
professionals employed in the theatre.[277] The piece sung was an original setting
of a song entitled '*Del dispotico potere*' ('Of despotic power'), with a text
celebrating the 1789 Declaration of the Rights of Men by the celebrated
Calabrian poet Luigi Rossi, which can be found throughout the triennium
1796–9 in various cities of the Italian peninsula and isles.[278] The fact that, in
July 1796, the French-occupied Italian states had already produced at least two
settings of a patriotic song dedicated to a French revolutionary event gives us an
insight into the pace of production and circulation of newly informed musical
products. Finally, musical performances were juxtaposed with other performative arts (here, spoken theatre) and encouraged the attendees' active participation (here, through dance).

Among the main foreign models to be embedded in local musical production
and soundscape were patriotic tunes, variously labelled as *chansons*, *hymnes*
and *chants*, and destined to be both sung and danced. Brought to Northern Italy
thanks to the mobility occasioned by the warfare, tunes popular in France since
the early 1790s, such as the *Carmagnole*, *Marseillaise* and *Ça ira*, quickly
became a constant of Milan's urban soundscape. Programmes, descriptions and
images of the festivals, as well as reports of the patriotic clubs' *séances*,

---

[276] Criscuolo, *Termometro politico della Lombardia*, vol. 1, p. 121.

[277] Chiappori, *Serie cronologica delle rappresentazioni drammatico-pantomimiche poste sulle
scene dei principali teatri di Milano 1776–1818*, p. 231.

[278] See, for example, *Campagna del gen. Buonaparte in Italia negli anni 4. e 5. della Repubblica
Francese . . .*, vol. 3 (Genoa: Stamperia delle Piane, 1798), pp. 15–16. F. Sulis, *Dei moti politici
dell'isola di Sardegna dal 1793 al 1821*, (Turin: Biancardi, 1857), pp. 35–8.

overflow with patriotic tunes sung by choirs or by the masses, played by military bands and/or with dancing around a Tree of Liberty.[279] The presence of these tunes went, however, far beyond their use in codified events: Salfi, for instance, publicly encouraged the common people to learn and sing them with the same zeal as prayers in the church.[280] An eyewitness also recalls how the *Chant du depart* (composed by Étienne Méhul on a text by Chénier in 1794, and so popular that it was called '*frère de La Marseillaise*', the *Marseillaise*'s brother), was often played in the city's public gardens in order to provide an 'appropriate' background for those taking a stroll.[281] Similarly, the local Guardia nazionale performed military evolutions with the accompaniment of *canti patriottici* every week, either in the gardens or on the castle's esplanade.[282] Vernacular verses also comment on (or lament) the fact that patriotic songs were ubiquitous, either on their own or mixed with tunes coming from theatre pieces; on an average day, for instance, people could hear and see the following being performed:

... *ballarin, omen e donn balland*	... dancers, both men and women,
Fussen savi o pur porcon, cantand	Sober or drunk, singing
El Sairà, nos enfant de la Patrì,	The *Ça ira*, '*Allons, enfants de la Patrie*',
La Loduiska, la Carmagnola pel rest del dì.[283]	*La Lodoiska* and *La Carmagnola* all day long.

French tunes were thus regularly sung and danced in the streets of Milan, on this particular occasion together with excerpts from an unspecified work based on the subject of Lodoiska. Beloved by French and Italian (and, as a matter of fact, Austrian) audiences alike, the tale of bravery set in a country (Poland) struggling to achieve freedom had been set to music by Cherubini and Kreutzer, who had produced very popular operas in Paris in 1791. In Lombardy, Kreutzer's work (described as a 'commedia eroica... frammischiata di canti') had been premiered in Monza in 1793, while the subject had been presented in the form of a heroic ballet by choreographer Paolo Franchi in 1794 and 1797. An opera on

---

[279] See, for example, *Giornale storico della Repubblica Cisalpina dall'epoca della sua Libertà e Indipendenza*, ms, vol. 1 (S.Q+I.14), I-Ma, pp. 14–18. *Descrizione delle feste date in Milano a' 28 e 29 piovoso . . .*, pp. 4–5. De Castro, *Milano e la Repubblica Cisalpina giusta le poesie, le caricature . . .*, p. 117. Criscuolo, *Termometro politico della Lombardia*, vol. 1, p. 11 (5 July 1796), and vol. 2, p. 250 (2 May 1798).

[280] Criscuolo, *Termometro politico della Lombardia*, vol. 1, p. 105 (2 July 1796).

[281] A. Challamel, *La France et les Français à travers les siècles*, vol. 3 (Paris: F. Roy, 1884), p. 355. Granville, *Autobiography of A. B. Granville*, p. 17.

[282] Criscuolo, *Termometro politico della Lombardia*, vol. 1, p. 105 (23 August 1796).

[283] Fumagalli, *L' ultima messa celebrata nella chiesa della Rosa in Milano . . .*, p. 7.

the same subject by Simon Mayr had also been premiered in Venice in 1796, its overture performed in 1798 in La Cannobiana to welcome the new Commander Pouget.[284] While it is not clear which of these works is referenced here (arguably Franchi's ballet due to the dance element), these verses describe the unparalleled mixture of repertoires, the engagement of the common people, the transfer of French models and the ubiquity of such varied amalgamations in the city's soundscape and landscape.

In parallel with Parisian practices, patriotic tunes also entered theatrical buildings, being regularly performed as part of operatic and ballet soirees.[285] A 1798 *Rapporto* (report) produced by the Commissione sui Teatri (a governmental commission entrusted with the 'republican' restructuring of theatre practices) prescribed that patriotic music had to be played in between the acts of operas.[286] Semi-spontaneous performances of songs and tunes, often demanded by *clubbisti* or by French soldiers, had, however, been happening since much earlier than that. As already mentioned, a performance of the *Marseillaise* had been given in La Scala on the very evening of Napoleon's arrival, the tune's sound in the theatre embodying very visibly the city's change of rulers. Similarly, in 1798, Commander Pouget had interrupted the orchestra playing in La Cannobiana, snapped the leader's bow, arrested the impresario and ordered that only patriotic tunes, such as *Ça ira*, be performed. The presence of French republican tunes in the theatres must have been very domineering, as the evening after Pouget's outburst, some French officers, profiting from his absence, begged the orchestra to stop playing the *Carmagnole* because they could not bear to hear it yet another time.[287]

Finally, patriotic tunes were appended to, or even incorporated into, operas, occasioning an even deeper amalgamation of occasions and repertoires: a notable example is that of *L'astuta in amore*, a comic opera with music by V. Fioravanti and libretto by G. Palomba, which the French had already programmed for the 1796 autumn season. Very traditional in setting, the opera included a happy ending in which finding love was celebrated by all characters.

[284] A. Aureli, La Rossana (Milan: G. B. Bianchi, 1794), pp. 11–13. Jean E.B. Dejaure, *Lodoiska: commedia eroica in tre atti, frammischiata di canti... da rappre sentarsi nel Teatro di Monza l'autunno 1793* (Milan: Gaetano Motta, 1793). *Giornale storico della Repubblica Cisalpina dall'epoca della sua Libertà e Indipendenza*, ms, vol. 2 (S.Q+I.15), I-Ma, p. 153. W. Dean, *'Opera under the French Revolution'*, in *Proceedings of the RMA* 94 (1968), pp. 82–3.

[285] Pierre, *Les Hymnes et les Chansons de la Révolution*, pp. 9–11.

[286] [*Rapporto Commissione sui Teatri*], 9 February 1799, I-Mas, AGSP P. A., folder 17.

[287] *Giornale storico della Repubblica Cisalpina dall'epoca della sua Libertà e Indipendenza*, ms, vol. 2 (S.Q+I.15), I-Ma, pp. 155–6.

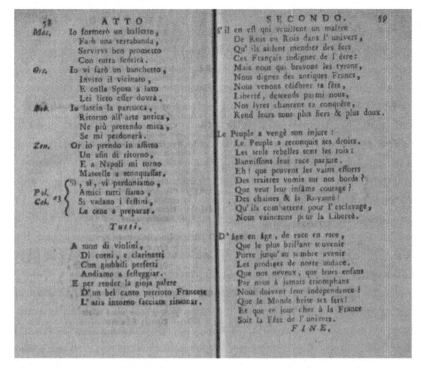

Figure 15 G. Palomba, *L'astuta in amore* (1796), Act-II finale.

© Ministero della Cultura – Pinacoteca di Brera – Biblioteca Braidense, Milan.

The libretto shows, however, how a French hymn, namely Lebrun's and Cherubini's *Chant républicain du 10 août* (1795), was inserted into this final scene: all characters on stage suddenly declare how '*un bel canto patriottico francese*' ('a nice French patriotic song')' is the best way to rejoice, and start singing the hymn in French (Figure 15).[288] However, no other editions of the libretto (even in other French-occupied cities, e.g. Bergamo) or the contemporary score bear any trace of Cherubini's hymn, but rather show a very traditional finale.[289] This seems to suggest that insertions such as this, already common on the Parisian stages, were quickly agreed upon, leaving no permanent musical evidence, and that they relied on the theatre artists' familiarity with the repertoire of French republican tunes, performed mainly from memory.[290]

---

[288] G. Palomba, *L'astuta in amore* (Milan: G. B. Bianchi, 1796), I-Mb, pp. 58–9.

[289] See, for example, G. Palomba, *L'astuta in amore* (Ferrara: Rinaldi, 1796), I-BGc; G. Palomba, *L'astuta in amore* (Bergamo: n.n., 1797), I-BGc; G. Palomba *L'astuta in amore* (Turin: F. Buzan, 1801), I-Bc; and V. Fioravanti, *L'astuta in amore*, ms score (1796), Noseda I.43–4, I-Mc, vol. 2, Finale.

[290] See, for example, J. Dracon, *Chanson patriotique chantée ... sur le théâtre de la République* (n.d.), YE-55471, F-Pn (1787).

Because of the ephemerality of many practices implemented by the republican regimes, the lack of systematic evidence makes it difficult to establish how
often such events took place; it is undoubtable, however, that French patriotic
songs became a constant of Milan's soundscape in many different occasions and
venues, and a staple of political communication and engagement. Considered
one of the most successful products of the Revolution, these tunes also contributed to the introduction of a particularly aggressive use of music, used to
express polarized political ideas (e.g. hatred towards the recent past), as well
as the activism advocated by the revolutionaries.[291] Drawing on the proximity
with the French language, some tunes also became so closely associated with
republican activism that they were used as political slogans: a *Stemma* (coat of
arms) designed in 1797 by the demagogue Giuseppe Ranza for the Piedmontese
patriots, for instance, portrays all major French revolutionary symbols (e.g. the
Tree of Liberty and the tricoloured flag), accompanied by a series of medallions
with slogans in Italian alternated with *Ça ira* (Figure 16).

Another model coming from revolutionary France was that of the instrumental
pieces commissioned for the Parisian festivals, which were imported into Lombardy
through both printed musical materials and actual performances within festivals and
other celebrations.[292] The presence of French military corps and their bands also
guaranteed the appropriate level of exposure in terms of styles and practices while
the military corps of the Cisalpine Republic (e.g. the Cisalpine army and the Guardia
nazionale) developed their own bands.[293] Milan lacked institutions such as the
Parisian École Royale de Chant, the École de Musique de la Garde Nationale and
(from 1796) the Paris Conservatoire, where composers and performers were trained
in the composition and performance of the music needed for patriotic celebration.[294]
Much of the music requested for festivals evoked the military sphere, articulating the
strong association between Napoleon and war power, and (in Milan) between the
military achievements of the Armée d'Italie and Lombardy's newly found freedom.
Marches and funeral and battle music also functioned very well in conjunction with
the parades, weapon exhibitions and military sounds used in many celebrations, and
were systematically embedded in different venues/occasions: at a patriotic banquet
in 1797, for instance, the military band of the Guardia nazionale in the National
(former Ducal) Palace could be seen performing together with two cannons positioned in the nearby cathedral square in almost antiphonal style.[295]

---

[291] Moiraghi, *Napoleone a Milano*, p. 15. Mason, *Singing the French Revolution*, p. 35.

[292] Pierre, *Musique des fêtes et cérémonies de la Révolution française*, pp. LXXVIII–IX.

[293] Rota, '*Milano napoleonica*', p. 63. Moiraghi, *Napoleone a Milano*, p. 58.

[294] C. M. Gessele, 'The Conservatoire de Musique and National Music Education in France, 1795–
    1801', in *Music and the French Revolution*, ed. by M. Boyd (Cambridge: Cambridge University
    Press, 1992), pp. 198–9.

[295] *Descrizione delle feste date in Milano a' 28 e 29 piovoso . . .*, p. 5.

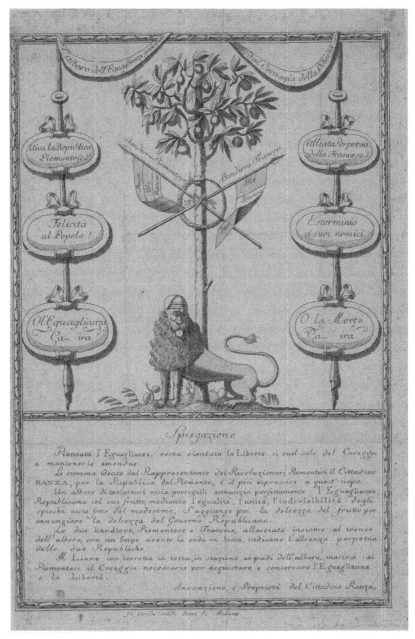

Figure 16 G. Ranza, 'Stemma repubblicano' (1797).
© Civica Raccolta delle Stampe 'Achille Bertarelli', Castello Sforzesco, Milano.

Finally, a strong link was established between military sounds/music and patriotic songs. In the festival organized in the autumn of 1797 to celebrate the most recent victories of the French army, for instance, the handing of the flag from one corps to the other was accompanied by the following elements to be performed in exact succession and conjunction with visual gestures:

1. Trumpet fanfare
2. Drum roll
3. *Ça ira* played by the band of the Guardia nazionale
4. *Marseillaise* played by two unspecified orchestras.[296]

The lyrics of many songs also made direct references to warfare, weapons and military sounds, channelling the people's enthusiasm in a very aggressive direction; notable examples include the celebrated '*aux armes, citoyens*!' from the *Marseillaise* and the '*vive le son du cannon*' from the *Carmagnole*. At the same time, republican propaganda and the press promoted popular engagement, fuelled by patriotic music, through individual, often violent, actions and through enlistment in the newly founded 'national' army.[297]

The republican regime's musical needs could also rely on the intense musical scene taking place in the two opera houses, as well as in the numerous churches, salons and aristocratic palaces, which caused a notable number of artists to live or regularly sojourn in Milan. Like their Parisian counterparts, many Milan-based composers, librettists and musicians had to reorient their activities towards the new needs and frames of musical production. The process of commissioning and producing music changed dramatically from what many artists were used to, as did the nature of the musical products required, the music's purpose and the requested juxtaposition of local and foreign repertoires. A series of musical performances organized in May 1797 as part of the celebrations for the *Campagne d'Italie*'s first anniversary, which was relatively well documented through administrative outputs such as invoices and correspondence, allows us to observe the interplay between these processes. Firstly (possibly because of the 'Italian' focus of the celebration), a team of local artists, mainly employed in La Scala, was appointed to provide almost all of the music needed: the poet and librettist Adelemo Fugazza supplied several poems of strongly patriotic content, while the composers and musicians Ambrogio Minoja, Alessandro Rolla and Luigi de Bailou had to set the texts provided to music moulded around several French models, rearrange operatic numbers and supply pieces for instrumentalists (both orchestra and military-band players). The letter of appointment was sent to Minoja and Rolla (chosen mainly for their 'patriotic zeal') on 29 April, just a few days before

---

[296] *Descrizione delle feste date in Milano a' 28 e 29 piovoso* ..., p. 4
[297] See, for example, Criscuolo, *Termometro politico della Lombardia*, vol. 1, p. 262 (27 August 1796).

the start of the celebrations (4 May), mirroring the working conditions of many Parisian artists, and confirming their role as government employees.[298] The extremely fast work pace also caused the music to retain a very occasional character, arguably contributing (together with its highly propagandistic value) to its ultimate disappearance. The list of works supplied and their performance specifics can be see in Table 2.

The cross-contamination between French and Italian models, performers and skills can be clearly seen, as can the attention placed on grand performances with a very engaging character: operatic numbers (in this case, Paisiello's chorus), for instance, were rescored for outdoor performances, involving greater musical forces and mirroring the parallel process of patriotic pieces being inserted in and adapted for operatic soirees. In terms of the newly supplied choral music, while the labels used by Minoja are rather unclear, his pieces were probably based around two of the most popular types produced in revolutionary France: a more antiphonal chorus with soloists and choral responses and a more solemn chorus to be sung either in unison or by whole sections alternating; the latter was probably also similar to Cherubini's *Chant républicain*, performed not so long before (Autumn 1796) in La Scala. Thanks to an angry letter that Minoja sent to the

Table 2 List of works performed at the celebrations in May 1797

Piece	Performance venue(s)	Performers
I. Concertato chorus A. Minoja	1. La Scala	Twenty-five choristers Twelve players
	2. Outdoors (Palazzo Serbelloni)	The above plus a military band (twelve extra players)
II. Final chorus from *Il re Teodoro in Venezia* G. Paisiello arr. A. Rolla	Outdoors (unspecified)	Choir and orchestra (La Scala)
III. Patriotic hymn A. Minoja	Outdoors (Porta Romana)	Twenty-five choristers Thirty-six players
IV. Symphonies, marches L. de Bailou	Outdoors (unspecified)	Military bands and extra players[299]

---

[298] [Letter Commissione per le Feste to Ambrogio Minoja], 29 April 1797, I-Mas, AGSP P.A., folder 2.

[299] *Ibid.* [Invoice], manuscript, n.d., I-Mas, AGSP P.A., folder 2.

Commissione after the celebrations to urge payment, we also know that the pieces were centred on 'local' topics (i.e. Napoleon's victories in the Italian campaign and Lombardy's freedom).[300] The *sinfonie e marce* supplied by the Milan-born but Paris-trained de Bailou also followed the well-codified French model of instrumental music with a military twist. Many artists quickly adapted to this system, which allowed them to not only survive but also thrive. The most notable example is that of Minoja, who, thanks to his ability to adapt and supply specific musical products, managed to be successfully employed throughout the republican and monarchical regimes, and even after the Restoration.[301]

Finally, the already mentioned 1801 festival organized to celebrate the establishment of the second Cisalpine Republic and the Foro Bonaparte's construction, gives a deeper insight into the juxtaposition between musical, sonic and visual elements to maximize their power for ritualization, communication and engagement. The festival, arguably the very last of its kind and scale before a shift towards the cult of the individual (Napoleon) and the monarchical regime, can be considered a synthesis of the public-celebration practices implemented in Milan throughout its two republican experiences. By cross-checking the pamphlets printed for the occasion, as well as by looking at contemporary iconography, we can reconstruct in detail the succession of choreographed movements/gestures together with their musical and sonic accompaniment (Table 3).

The concert of different performing arts, visual and sonic elements, artists and repertoires within a highly theatralized space and time fully realized the model proposed by the revolutionary theorists in terms of both solemnization and public education/engagement. While events on such a scale were relatively rare, many elements embedded in their frame, from the republican tunes to the military sounds, permeated Milan's urban soundscape and landscape on a deeper level, modifying the people's daily experience and perception. At the same time, the collaboration between artists and institutions across venues and performance spaces occasioned the thinning down of many boundaries traditionally separating them and impressed a significant acceleration on Milan's dramatic/performative world. While the end of the second Cisalpine Republic (1802) and of the more moderate Italian Republic (1805) signalled the end of these celebrations, many of their components had already planted a seed within Milan's self-perception and ideal imagery; the city had in fact become not only

---

[300] [Letter Ambrogio Minoja to the Commissione per le Pubbliche Feste], manuscript, n.d, I-Mas, AGSP P.A., folder 2.

[301] A. Palidda, 'Milan and the Music of Political Transitions in the Napoleonic Period . . .', in *Music and War in Europe from the French Revolution to WWI*, ed. by E. Jardin (Turnhout, Belgium: Brepols, 2016), pp. 105–22.

Table 3 Visual and sonic choreography for the 1801 festival

Event/gesture	Music/sound	'Performers'
Arrival of the *cortège* in the Forum	Gunfire	Soldiers
The *cortège* takes place in the amphitheatre	Patriotic speech (*Sulla Pace* by G. Compagnoni)	Speaker (G. Compagnoni)
The civil and military officers climb the stairs leading to the amphitheatre; boys present them with olive branches	Symphonies	Unspecified (orchestra and choir of La Scala and bands)
	Inno patriottico, music by A. Minoja, words by A. Petracchi	
	Chorus, music by L. de Bailou, words by A. Petracchi	
Officers move towards the funeral monument	Funeral march	Unspecified (see above)
Officers reach the funeral monument; boys drape it with wreaths of flowers	Military sounds and evolutions	Soldiers
Officers move towards the Temple of Immortality	Joyful march	Unspecified (see above)
Officers reach the temple; boys hang wreaths of laurel on the temple's columns	Explosions from the castle's ruins	Soldiers

Table 3 (cont.)

Event/gesture	Music/sound	'Performers'
Officers go back to the amphitheatre; solemn commemoration of the fallen soldiers	Patriotic speech La Pace by V. Monti Reading of the inscription on the foundation stone	Civic and military authorities
Laying of the foundation stone	Military instruments and sounds	Soldiers
Evening feast in La Scala	Cantata Il trionfo della pace, music by F. Pollini, libretto by A. Fugazza Festa da ballo[302]	Choir and orchestra of La Scala Three soloists

[302] Programma della festa per la celebrazione della pace . . . . P. Lonati, Description de la fête qui a eu lieu le 10 Floréal an 9 . . . (Milan: n.n., 1801). A. Fugazza, Il trionfo della pace (Milan: n.n., 1801). A. Petracchi, Coro . . . posto in musica dal cittadino Baillou da cantarsi in occasione della festa del 10 fiorile anno 9 (Milan: n.n., 1801), I-Mb. A. Petracchi, Inno patriottico . . . posto in musica dal cittadino Minoja da cantarsi in occasione della festa del 10 Fiorile anno 9 (Milan: n.n., 1801), I-Mc. G. Compagnoni, Sulla pace . . . (Milan: Stamperia Iitaliana e Francese a S. Zeno, 1801). V. Monti, La pace . . . (Milan: n.n., 1801), all in I-Mb, Misc. KK.IV.10.

a powerhouse of politically informed culture but also a political theatre *tout court*, where concepts and ideas were continuously staged and performed.

Many features of Milan's republican landscape and soundscape can, indeed, be found in the city's militarization and urban riots of later decades. The use of music, sounds/noises and visual elements for specific engagement and educational purposes linked to political activism had planted fruitful seeds in musical production, especially regarding musical theatre. At the same time, the relationship between sound/music, urban space and active participation connected to patriotic sentiments (albeit artificial ones) had become stronger, laying the foundation for many social and political behaviours of the following decades. Frequently dismissed as extreme and idiosyncratic displays of propaganda, the festivals and celebrations organized in republican Milan can, indeed, be considered an experience that exerted a strong influence on the city's present and immediate future on a plurality of levels.

Epilogue
Between Square and Theatre

As shown in the previous sections, republican festivals implemented in Milan by adapting revolutionary models to the local specificities had strong consequences for the city's landscape and soundscape, as well as for inhabitants' daily experience and perception. Both the public spaces and sonorous dimension were permeated by a series of carefully codified products and practices, which were as rich as they are hard to label and which occasioned intense immersive experiences. These experiences occasioned and, at the same time, resulted from a series of unparalleled encounters that widened the bases for cultural production and consumption, and projected Milan into the fast-paced post-Restoration period. The high degree of engagement/activism and the politicized communication embedded in the republican celebrations, as well as in their wider frame (e.g. the press and clubs), can be considered, indeed, features that had a significant impact on the perceptions and attitudes of the Milanese. At the same time, festivals and other celebratory events advocated another idea that the Milanese society and artists would develop further, that music and sound (often with visuals/an embedded narrative) could become effective tools of public education, especially in the case of developing hatred and engagement against a supposedly oppressive system. In this sense, an overview of the main features of musical theatre and theatre management in Napoleonic Milan offers the opportunity not only to observe yet another sphere on which the republican years had a strong impact but also to formulate further comments on the blurring of the boundaries between performance venues and public space, and between theatrical and political practices.

The opera house was much more controlled and traditional than any other performance space, with the sole exception of religious ones; this was particularly true in the case of Milan, where the local aristocracy exerted unparalleled control on theatrical space and management, making La Scala a difficult space to penetrate. With opera remaining a paramount form of entertainment and gathering for the local aristocracy (who had to be involved in the process of general regeneration), republican authorities had to devise a system to penetrate that sphere, and to bring it closer to the public space of action.[1] Theatres also had to be appropriated by the revolutionary cause because of their strong association with the synergy between

---

[1] M. Nocciolini, '*Il melodramma nella Milano napoleonica . . .*', in *Nuova rivista musicale italiana* 29/1 (1995), p. 5. C. Toscani, '*Politica culturale e teatro nell'Italia napoleonica . . .*', in *L'aere è fosco, il ciel s'imbruna . . .*, ed. by F.Passadore and F. Rossi (Venice: Edizioni Fondazione Levi, 2000), pp. 72–5.

Austrian rulers and Milanese citizens, embedded in their very layout.[2] Furthermore, musical theatre, with its refined combination of visuals, music and emotion-driven plots, was a potentially effective tool of communication of republican morals: it was also easy to draw on the familiarity that theatre patrons already had with subjects and characters from antiquity, which offered a vast pool of resources.[3]

Numerous attempts were made to democratize the theatrical space, from the plans (never realized) of destroying the Palchettone to make way for individual boxes, to the transfer of all boxes that had been left empty to the public.[4] At the same time, entry prices were significantly lowered, with performances of high patriotic value even given free of charge. Members of the lower bourgeoisie, shopkeepers and artisans dressed in everyday clothes attended the performances with increasing frequency, so that the queues to enter the theatre became longer than ever, and the number of benches in the stalls had to be continuously increased.[5] For the first time, it was the varied audience sitting in the stalls that initiated the applause and demanded encores without asking for approval from or waiting for the aristocrats in the boxes: the relation between audience, perform-ance space and behaviour, already strong in Milan, became even more difficult to control.[6] While these measures were motivated by a clear propagandistic purpose and caused painful contrasts with the impresario, *palchettisti* and artists, they can also be seen as weakening or abolishing many old privileges that made the theatrical system rather stagnant (e.g. the so-called *convenienze teatrali*).[7]

In terms of performance material, the Milanese theatres saw the systematic juxtaposition and amalgamation of different repertoires and features on a completely different scale from the few, highly standardized cantatas and *feste teatrali* performed during the Habsburg rule. These juxtapositions ranged from the already mentioned performances of patriotic tunes within operatic frames or at the audience's semi-spontaneous request, to large-scale instrumen-tal and vocal works commissioned and produced specifically for republican celebration. Two notable examples are those of the funeral symphony *La morte*

---

[2] Bianchi, 'Space and Hegemony at La Scala, 1776–1850s', pp. 1–2.

[3] A. Paglicci Brozzi, *Sul teatro giacobino ed antigiacobino in Italia* (Milan: Pirola, 1887), vol. 1, p. 42. C. Toscani, '*Soggetti romantici nell'opera italiana del periodo napoleonico*', in *Aspetti dell'opera italiana fra Sette e Ottocento* . . ., ed. by G. Salvetti (Lucca: LIM, 1993), p. 13.

[4] [Report Minister of Internal Affairs], 9 February 1799, [Letter Minister of Internal Affairs to the Directory] and [Letter Directory to the National Treasury], 20 April 1799, all in I-Mas, AGSP P. A., folder 17.

[5] Tintori, *Duecento anni alla Scala*, p. 14. V. Ferrari, *Il Teatro della Scala nella vita e nell'arte* . . ., p. 20.

[6] Bianchi, 'Space and Hegemony at La Scala, 1776–1850s', p. 735.

[7] [*Rapporto della Commissione sui Teatri*], 1 June 1798, I-Mc, FS, folder 2. B. Andreoli, [*Regolamento*], n.d. (1798), I-Mas, AGSP P.A., folder 17. Giazotto, *Le carte della Scala*, pp. 33–7. Cambiasi, *La Scala 1778–1889*, pp. 31–4.

del Generale Hoche (*The Death of General Hoche*), performed in April 1798,
and the *Inno per l'anniversario della caduta dell'ultimo Re dei Francesi Luigi
XVI* (*Hymn for the Anniversary of the Fall of the last French King Louis XVI*),
from January 1799, both with music by Minoja.

The symphony was the winner of nationwide competition of patriotic music,
the first event of its kind in Milan;[8] the score shows the merging of features
coming from the French revolutionary pieces with some already in use in the
theatre, producing yet another relevant encounter.[9] The hymn made use not only
of Minoja's experience with music for republican celebration but also of lyrics
by one of the most successful poets of the Napoleonic period, Vincenzo Monti.
Monti displayed a particularly inflamed rhetoric and vivid images, using a tone
very close to that of republican oratory; with the music being lost, the libretto
also reveals that the piece needed three soloists (including the celebrated
soprano Elizabeth Billington), a choir of twenty-eight and an orchestra of sixty-
one, adhering to the model of the French *hymnes à grand coeur* that were
regularly performed in both the theatre and festivals.[10]

Finally, La Scala saw a plethora of 'republican' subjects chosen for the operas
and ballets offered; its Parisian counterparts had already carried out years of
experimenting with appropriate matters, selecting several episodes in both
ancient classical and recent national history that could showcase typically
republican values and virtues, and fostering a fruitful cross-fertilization
between spoken and musical theatre.[11] Opere serie were especially used for
their dramatic narrative and representation of tragic heroes, but appropriate
settings and frames also turned ballets and opere buffe into useful tools of
'morally appropriate' entertainment. While the control of subject matter is by
no means a novelty, it is interesting to point out that many of these 'republican
stage works' implemented features coming from contemporary extra-theatrical
musical performances. The most evident is the systematic use of choral masses,
often symbolizing the union and strong will either of the whole people or of
groups characterized by noble purposes; this shift from individual to collective

---

[8] [Annoucement], 6 November 1797, I-Ms, MAN 2998. Chiappori, *Serie cronologica delle rappresentazioni drammatico-pantomimiche . . .*, pp. 58–9. Cambiasi, *La Scala 1778–1889*, p. 31.

[9] A. Minoja, *La Morte del Generale Hoche. Sinfonia a Grande Orchestra*, ms score, MAYR Fald.
251/4, I-BGc.

[10] V. Monti, *Inno per l'anniversario della caduta dell'ultimo Re dei Francesi Luigi XVI*, ms, I-Mc,
FS, folder 2. See also Cambiasi, *La Scala 1778–1889*, p. 34. Bosisio, '*Un poeta al servizio di un
nuovo modello di spettacolo*', p. 251.

[11] E. C. Bartlet, 'The New Repertory of the Opéra during the Reign of Terror', in *Music and the
French Revolution*, ed. by M. Boyd (Cambridge: Cambridge University Press, 1992), pp. 110–
12. R. Ketterer, 'Roman Republicanism and Operatic Heroines in Napoleonic Italy . . .', in
Operatic Migrations, ed. by R. Montemorra Marvin and D. A. Thomas (Burlington: Ashgate,
2006), pp. 98–9.

sentiments and actions was already present in many Parisian operas of the 1790s and mirrored many festival pieces/gestures.[12]

Another relevant element used across all genres of musical theatre was the replication on stage of visual structures and settings used in the festivals, bringing the theatralized urban space, as well as the music, into the theatre itself. Trees of Liberty, military barracks, communal halls and temples dedicated to allegorical deities featured in many settings, often regardless of their historical or geographical location.[13] A similar, bidirectional process can be observed in terms of sound: while La Scala's orchestra and chorus, as already shown, often performed alongside military band musicians in outdoor celebrations, republican tunes, military symbols and band instruments found their way onto the theatrical stage and orchestra thanks to the abundance of military heroes, war settings and solemn choral scenes. Both processes have also been well documented on the Parisian stages, but can be considered even more interesting in the context of Milan because of the transnational nature of this encounter.[14]

Even a very general look at theatre practices in Milan during the Napoleonic years reveals how the proximity between the theatrical and public spaces and the links between theatre and urban stages significantly increased. While often dismissed as scarcely documented occasional and propagandistic works, the operas and ballets produced at La Scala throughout the republican years allow us to establish yet another layer of comparative observation, and to confirm that celebratory musical practices had a strong impact on Milan seen not only as a physical and resounding space but also as a producer of music and culture with a specific identity and impact on future experiences.

---

[12] Traversier, "*Transformer la plèbe en* peuple'", pp. 55–6. Tocchini, '*Dall'antico regime alla Cisalpina* . . .', pp. 57–8.

[13] See, for example, F. S. Salfi, *La congiura pisoniana* (Milan: G. B. Bianchi, 1797), I-Ms, p. 23. *La città nuova* (Milan: G. B. Bianchi, 1798), p. 7.

[14] 'The New Repertory of the Opéra during the Reign of Terror', p. 133. D. Wiles, *Theatre and Citizenship. The History of a Practice* (Cambridge: Cambridge University Press, 2014), p. 151–2.

List of RISM Library Sigla Used

F-Pn	Bibliothèque nationale de France, Département de la Musique, Paris
GB-Lbl	The British Library, London
I-Bc	Museo internazionale e biblioteca della musica, Bologna
I-BGc	Biblioteca civica 'Angelo Mai' e Archivi storici comunali, Bergamo
I-Ma	Biblioteca Ambrosiana, Milan
I-Mas	Archivio di Stato, Milan
I-Mb	Biblioteca Nazionale Braidense, Milan
I-Mc	Biblioteca del Conservatorio Statale di Musica 'Giuseppe Verdi', Milan
I-Mrsb	Civica Raccolta delle Stampe 'Achille Bertarelli', Milan
I-Mts	Biblioteca teatrale 'Livia Simoni' del Museo Teatrale alla Scala, Milan
I-MZc	Biblioteca civica, Monza
I-Ra	Biblioteca Angelica, Rome

References

1 Archival Sources

Atti di Governo, Spettacoli Pubblici (AGSP), *Parte Antica*, folders 1–6, I-Mas.

Fondo Somma (FS), folders 1–6, I-Mc.

Giornale storico della Repubblica Cisalpina dall'epoca della sua Libertà e Indipendenza, ms, 6 vols. (S. Q.+. I. 14–19), I-Ma.

D. A. Minola, *Diario storico politico di alcuni avvenimenti del secolo XVIII*, ms, 14 vols., G 111–124 suss, I-Ma.

Salazar (SAL) and Manifesti (MAN) folders, I-Ms.

Miscellaneous collections: Misc.1416.D.13, Misc. 1416.E.1 and Misc. KK. IV.10, I-Mb.

2 Librettos and Scores

A. Aureli, *La Rossana* . . . (Milan: G. B. Bianchi, 1794), I-Mb.

L. Da Ponte, *Le nozze di Figaro. Commedia per musica da rappresentarsi nel Teatro di Monza l'autunno dell'anno 1787* (Milan: G. B. Bianchi, 1787), I-MZc.

Jean E.B. Dejaure, *Lodoiska: commedia eroica in tre atti, frammischiata di canti . . . da rappresentarsi nel Teatro di Monza l'autunno 1793* (Milan: Gaetano Motta, 1793).

J. Dracon, *Chanson patriotique chantée . . . sur le théâtre de la République* (n.d.), YE-55471, F-Pn.

V. Fioravanti, *L'astuta in amore*, ms score (1796), Noseda I.43–4, I-Mc.

A. Fugazza, *Il trionfo della pace* (Milan: n.n., 1801), I-Mb.

F.-J. Gossec, *Le Triomphe de la République ou Le Camp de Grand Pré*, libretto by M.-J. Chénier (Paris: Huguet, n.d.), F-Pn.

Te Deum, ms score (1790), MS-1430, F-Pn.

La città nuova (Milan: G. B. Bianchi, 1798), I-Mb.

P. Metastasio, *Il Ruggiero ovvero L'eroica gratitudine* (Rome: N. Barbiellini, 1771), I-Ra.

A. Minoja, *La Morte del Generale Hoche. Sinfonia a Grande Orchestra*, ms score, MAYR Fald. 251/4, I-BGc.

G. Palomba, *L'astuta in amore* (Ferrara: Rinaldi, 1796), I-BGc.

L'astuta in amore (Milan: G. B. Bianchi, 1796), I-Mb.

L'astuta in amore (Bergamo: n.n., 1797), I-BGc.

L'astuta in amore (Turin: F. Buzan, 1801), I-Bc.

G. Parini, *Ascanio in Alba* (Milan: G. B. Bianchi, 1771), I-Mb.

A. Petracchi, *Coro ... posto in musica dal cittadino Baillou da cantarsi in occasione della festa del 10 fiorile anno 9* (Milan: n.n., 1801), I-Mb.

Inno patriottico ... posto in musica dal cittadino Minoja da cantarsi in occasione della festa del 10 Fiorile anno 9 (Milan: n.n., 1801), I-Mc.

G. Riviera, *La Gara dei geni nel felice nascimento del Serenissimo arciduca d'Austria Pietro Leopoldo* (Milan: G. P. Malatesta, 1747), I-Mb.

F. S. Salfi, *La congiura pisoniana* (Milan: G. B. Bianchi, 1797), I-Ms.

A. Salvi, *La Germania trionfante in Arminio* (Milan: G. P. Malatesta, 1739), I-Bc.

M. Verazi, *Europa riconosciuta* (Milan: G. B. Bianchi, 1778), I-Mb.

3 Bibliographical Sources

Almanacco italiano e francese per l'anno 1796 ... (Milan: F. Bolzani, 1796).

Annali della Fabbrica del Duomo di Milano dall'origine fino al presente, vol. 6 (Milan: E. Reggiani, 1885).

H. Arendt, *On Revolution* (New York: Viking Press, 1963).

D. Aspari, *Vedute di Milano* (Milan: n.n., 1792), Plate 15.

C. Balbo, *Sommario della storia d'Italia dalle origini fino ai nostri tempi* (Turin: UTET, 1860).

E. Balmas, 'Dalla festa di corte alla festa giacobina', in *Lo spettacolo nella Rivoluzione francese*, ed. by P. Bosisio (Rome: Bulzoni, 1989), pp. 137–55.

A. Banti, *Il Risorgimento italiano*, 4th ed. (Rome: Laterza, 2004).

F. Barbieri, R. Carpani and A. Mignatti (eds.), *Festa, rito e teatro nella gran città di Milano*, exhibition catalogue, Milan, Pinacoteca Ambrosiana, 24 November 2009–28 February 2010 (Milan: Biblioteca Ambrosiana, 2010).

E. C. Bartlet, 'The New Repertory of the Opéra during the Reign of Terror: Revolutionary Rhetoric and Operatic Consequences', in *Music and the French Revolution*, ed. by M. Boyd (Cambridge: Cambridge University Press, 1992), pp. 107–56.

F. Bascialli, *Opera comica e opéra comique al Teatro Arciducale di Monza (1778–1795)* (Lucca: LIM, 2002).

A. Bassi, *La musica in Lombardia nel 1700* (Bologna: Forni, 1992).

D. Beales, *Enlightenment and Reform in Eighteenth-Century Europe* (London: I. B. Tauris & Co., 2005).

C. Bernardi and C. Bini, 'Ragionevoli culti ...', in *La cultura della rappresentazione nella Milano del Settecento*, ed. by R. Carpani, A. Cascetta and D. Zardin (Rome: Bulzoni, 2010), pp. 445–94.

A. Bertarelli and A. Monti (eds.), *Tre secoli di vita Milanese* (Milan: Hoepli, 1927).

C. Bessonnet-Favre, *Les fêtes républicaines depuis 1789 jusqu'à nos jours* (Paris: Gedalge, 1909).

G. Bezzola and G. Tintori, *I protagonisti e l'ambiente della Scala nell'età neoclassica* (Milan: Il Polifilo, 1984).

R. Bianchi, 'Space and Hegemony at La Scala, 1776–1850s', in *The European Legacy* 18/4 (2013), pp. 730–74.

C. Bithell, 'The Past in Music: Introduction', in *Ethnomusicology Forum* 15/1 (2006), pp. 3–16.

A. Bosisio, *Storia di Milano* (Milan: Giunti-Martello, 1958).

P. Bosisio, '*Introduzione*', in *Lo spettacolo nella Rivoluzione francese*, ed. by P. Bosisio (Rome: Bulzoni, 1989), pp. 7–8.

'*Un poeta al servizio di un nuovo modello di spettacolo …*', in *Vincenzo Monti nella cultura italiana*, ed. by G. Barbarisi and W. Spaggiari, vol. 3 (Milan: Cisalpino, 2006), pp.245–61.

C.-M. Bosséno, '*Le feste civiche*', in *L'Italia nella Rivoluzione, 1789–1799*, exhibition catalogue, Rome, Biblioteca nazionale centrale, 6 March– 7 April, ed. by G. Benassati and L. Rossi (Bologna: Grafis, 1990), pp. 69–74.

R. Buclon, '*Napoléon et Milan. Mise en scène, réception et délégation du pouvoir napoléonien (1796–1814)*', PhD dissertation, Université de Grenoble and Università degli studi di Napoli Federico II, 2014.

C. Burney, *The Present State of Music in France and Italy*, 2nd ed. (London: T. Becket & Co., 1773).

P. Cambiasi, *La Scala 1778–1889: note storiche e statistiche* (Milan: Ricordi, 1889).

Campagna del gen. Buonaparte in Italia negli anni 4. e 5. della Repubblica Francese …, vol. 3 (Genoa: Stamperia delle Piane, 1798).

M. Canella, '*Aspetti e figure della cultura milanese nel percorso verso la modernità*', in *Il laboratorio della modernità*, ed. by Carlo Capra (Milan: Skira, 2003), pp. 79–89.

P. Canguilhelm, 'Courtiers and Musicians Meet in the Streets: The Florentine *Mascherata* under Cosimo I', in *Urban History* 37/3 (2010), pp. 464–73.

C. Cantù, *Storia della letteratura italiana* (Florence: Le Monnier, 1865).

C. Capra, '*Austriaci e francesi a Milano*', in *Il laboratorio della modernità*, ed. by Carlo Capra (Milan: Skira, 2003), pp. 13–19.

'*Milano al tempo di Giuseppe Parini*', in *La Milano del Giovin Signore*, ed. by F. Mazzocca and A. Morandotti (Milan: Skira, 1999), pp. 15–33.

'*Milano nell'età delle riforme*', in *Storia illustrata di Milano*, ed. by F. Della Peruta, vol. 5 (Milan: Sellino, 1993), pp. 1321–39.

A. Carlini, '*Lo strepitoso risonar de' stromenti da fiato & timballierie …*', in *L'aere è fosco, il ciel s'imbruna …*, ed. by F. Passadore and F. Rossi (Venice: Edizioni Fondazione Levi, 2000), pp. 473–505.

D. Carpanetto, *L'Italia del Settecento* (Turin: Loescher, 1980).

D. Carpanetto and G. Ricuperati, *Italy in the Age of Reason 1685–1789* (London: Longman, 1987).

R. Carpani, '*Introduzione*', in *Festa, rito e teatro nella gran città di Milano*, ed. by F. Barbieri, R. Carpani and A. Mignatti (Milan: Biblioteca Ambrosiana, 2010), pp. 892–3.

J. J. Carreras, 'Topography, Sound and Music . . .', in *Hearing the City in Early Modern Europe*, ed. by T. Knighton and A. Mazuela-Anguita (Turnhout, Belgium: Brepols, 2018), pp. 85–100.

T. Carter, 'Listening to Music in Early Modern Italy', in *Hearing the City in Early Modern Europe*, ed. by T. Knighton and A. Mazuela-Anguita (Turnhout, Belgium: Brepols, 2018), pp. 25–49.

'The Sound of Silence', in *Urban History* 29/1 (2002), pp. 8–18.

C. Cattaneo, *Notizie naturali e civili su la Lombardia*, vol. 1 (Milan: Giovanni Bernardoni, 1844).

F. Cazzamini Mussi, *Aneddoti milanesi* (Rome: Formiggini, 1932).

Il giornalismo a Milano dalle origini alla prima guerra di indipendenza (Milan: Famiglia meneghina, 1934).

C. Cerf and P. C. Hannesse, *Histoire et description de Notre-Dame . . .* (Reims: P. Dubois, 1861).

T. Ceva, *Relazione delle pubbliche feste fatte dalla città di Milano alli 7 di giugno 1716* (Milan: G. P. Malatesta, 1716).

A. Challamel, *La France et les Français à travers les siècles*, vol. 3 (Paris: F. Roy, 1884).

G. Chiappori, *Serie cronologica delle rappresentazioni drammatico-pantomimiche poste sulle scene dei principali teatri di Milano 1776–1818* (Milan: Silvestri, 1818).

F. Clément and P. Larousse, *Dictionnaire lyrique . . .* (Paris: Administration du grand dictionnaire universel, 1869).

Confédération Nationale . . . (Paris: Garnéry, 1790).

D. Costantini and A. Magaudda, 'Feste e cerimonie con musica nello Stato di Milano', in *Seicento inesplorato. L'evento musicale tra prassi e stile: un modello di interdipendenza*, ed. by A. Colzani, A. Luppi and M. Padoan (Como: A.M.I.S., 1993), pp. 65–94.

C. Cremonini, *Alla corte del Governatore . . .* (Rome: Bulzoni, 2012).

Le vie della distinzione . . . (Milan: EDUCatt, 2012).

M. A. Crippa and F. Zanzottero, *Le porte di Milano* (Milan: n.n., 1999).

V. Criscuolo (ed.), *Termometro politico della Lombardia* (Rome: Istituto storico italiano per l'età moderna e contemporanea, 1989).

S. Cuccia, *La Lombardia alla fine dell'Ancien Régime* (Florence: La Nuova Italia, 1971).

G. D'Amia, 'La città fatta teatro: apparati effimeri ed "embellissement" urbano ...', in *Il teatro a Milano nel Settecento*, ed. by A. Cascetta and G. Zanlonghi, vol. 1 (Milan: Vita e Pensiero, 2008), pp. 97–124.

D. Daolmi, 'Salfi alla Scala', in *Salfi librettista*, ed. by F. P. Russo (Vibo Valentia, Italy: Monteleone, 2001), pp. 133–77.

M. Darlow, *Staging the French Revolution* ... (Oxford: Oxford University Press, 2012).

W. Dean, 'Opera under the French Revolution', in *Proceedings of the RMA* 94 (1968), pp. 77–96.

C. De Brosses, *Lettres familières écrites d'Italie en 1739 et 1740* (Paris: Perrin, 1885).

G. De Castro, *Milano e la Repubblica Cisalpina giusta le poesie, le caricature* ... (Milan: F.lli Dumolard, 1879).

Milano nel Settecento (Milan: F.lli Dumolard, 1887).

G. De Finetti, *Milano. Costruzione di una città*, ed. by G. Cislaghi, M. De Benedetti, and P. Marabelli (Milan: Hoepli, 2002).

F. Degrada, 'Le esperienze milanesi di Mozart', in *L'amabil rito*, ed. by G. Barbarisi, C. Capra, F. Degrada, et al., vol. 2 (Bologna: Cisalpino, 2000), pp.731–50.

J. F. de La Harpe, *Du fanatisme dans la langue révolutionnaire* ... (Paris: Chaumerot, 1821).

N. Del Bianco, *Il coraggio e la sorte* (Milan: Franco Angeli, 1997).

Della instruzione nazionale ... (Cremona, Italy: Feraboli, 1799).

L. De Salvo and A. Sindoni (eds.), *Tempo sacro e tempo profano* (Soveria Mannelli, Italy: Rubbettino, 2002).

F. De Sanctis, *Storia della letteratura italiana* (Naples: Morano, 1870).

Descrizione delle feste date in Milano a' 28 e 29 piovoso ... (Milan: n.n., 1797).

Dettaglio, e spiegazione della festa federativa celebrata in Milano ... (Milan: Pulini al Bocchetto, 1797).

Discorso sui vantaggi del metodo col quale si è proclamata ... dalla Repubblica Francese la Cisalpina (Milan: Presso Luigi Veladini in contrada Santa Radegonda, 1797).

J.-P. Domecq, 'La Fête de l'Être suprême et son interprétation', in *Esprit* 154/9 (1989), pp. 91–125.

M. Donà, *Ascanio in Alba* (Lucca: LIM, 1997).

La musica a Milano nel Settecento durante la dominazione austriaca (unpublished typescript, n.d.), NUOVAMISC.A. 0643, I-Mb.

'Milan', in *The New Grove Dictionary of Music and Musicians*, ed. by S. Sadie and J. Tyrrell, vol. 5 (London: Macmillan, 1980), pp. 387–95.

W. Doyle, 'Introduction', in *The Oxford Handbook of the Ancien Régime*, ed. by W. Doyle (Oxford: Oxford University Press, 2011).

J. B. Duvergier, *Collection complete des lois, decrets, ordonnances* ..., vol. 6 (Paris: Guyot et Scribe, 1825).

A. Einstein, *Essays on Music* (London: Faber, 1958).

H. Engrand, *Leçons élémentaires sur l'Histoire de France* ... (Reims: Le Batard, 1816).

R.-A. Etlin, '*L'architecture et la fête de la féderation*', in *Les fêtes de la Révolution*, conference proceedings, Clermont Ferrand, France, 24–6 June, ed. by J. Ehrard and P. Viallaneix (Paris: Société des études robespierristes, 1974), pp. 131–54.

D. Fabris, 'Urban Musicologies', in *Hearing the City in Early Modern Europe*, ed. by T. Knighton and A. Mazuela-Anguita (Turnhout, Belgium: Brepols, 2018), pp. 53–68.

F. Fava, *Storia di Milano*, vol. 2 (Milan: Meravigli, 1981).

M. Feldman, *Opera and Sovereignty. Transforming Myths in Eighteenth-Century Italy* (Chicago: The University of Chicago Press, 2007).

V. Ferrari, *Il Teatro della Scala nella vita e nell'arte* ... (Milan: Tamburini, 1921).

S. Ferrone, '*La danse fut suspendue* ...', in *Lo spettacolo nella Rivoluzione francese*, ed. by P. Bosisio (Rome: Bulzoni, 1989), pp. 27–49.

G. B. Fumagalli, *L'ultima messa celebrata nella chiesa della Rosa in Milano* ... (Milan: Dall'autore contrada del Boschetto, n.d.).

F. Furet and M. Ozouf, *Dictionnaire critique de la Révolution française*, vol. 3, 2nd ed. (Paris: Flammarion, 2007).

G. Galbiati (ed.), *Il teatro alla Scala dagli inizi al 1794* (Milan: Biblioteca Ambrosiana, 1929).

G. Gargantini, *Cronologia di Milano* ... (Milan: Tipografia editrice lombarda, 1874).

C. M. Gessele, 'The Conservatoire de Musique and National Music Education in France, 1795–1801', in *Music and the French Revolution*, ed. by M. Boyd (Cambridge: Cambridge University Press, 1992), pp. 191–220.

R. Giazotto, *Le carte della Scala* (Pisa: Akademos, 1990).

J. Godechot, *La Grande Nation: l'expansion révolutionnaire de la France dans le monde* ..., 2nd ed. (Paris: A. Montaigne, 1983).

G. Gorani, *Storia di Milano dalla sua fondazione all'anno 1796* (Rome: Laterza, 1989).

A. Grab, *Napoleon and the Transformation of Europe* (Basingstoke: Palgrave Macmillan, 2003).

P. Granville (ed.), *Autobiography of A. B. Granville . . .*, vol. 1 (London: Henry S. King, 1874).

M. Graziano, *The Failure of Italian Nationhood . . .* (Basingstoke: Palgrave Macmillan, 2013).

P.-J. Grosley, *Observations sur l'Italie et les Italiens*, vol. 1 (London: n.n., 1770), p. 184.

K. Hansell, *Opera and Ballet at the Regio Ducal Teatro of Milan, 1771– 1776 . . .* (Ann Arbor: UMI, 1980).

P. R. Hanson, *Historical Dictionary of the French Revolution* (Lanham, MD: The Scarecrow Press, 2004).

F. W. J. Hemmings, *Culture and Society in France 1789–1848* (Leicester: Leicester University Press, 1987).

L. Hunt, *Politics, Culture, and Class in the French Revolution*, 2nd ed. (London: Methuen & Co., 1986).

I fasti repubblicani . . . (Milan: Pirola, 1802).

O. Ihl, *La fête républicaine*, ed. by M. Ozouf (Paris: Gallimard, 1996).

Il Corriere Milanese (Milan: Luigi Veladini in contrada S. Radegonda), 1(1793)- 4(1796).

Il giornale senza titolo, 46 (Milan: n.n., 1798).

C. Ingrao, *The Habsburg Monarchy 1618–1815* (Cambridge: Cambridge University Press, 1994).

R. L. Kendrick, *The Sounds of Milan, 1585–1650* (Oxford: Oxford University Press, 2002).

R. Ketterer, 'Roman Republicanism and Operatic Heroines in Napoleonic Italy . . .', in *Operatic Migrations*, ed. by R. Montemorra Marvin and D. A. Thomas (Burlington: Ashgate, 2006), pp. 99–124.

A. Körner, 'Beyond *Nationaloper . . .*', in *Journal of Modern Italian Studies* 25/ 4 (2020), pp. 402–19.

'National Movements against Nation States . . .', in *The 1848 Revolutions and European Political Thought*, ed. by D. Moggach and G. Stedman Jones (Cambridge: Cambridge University Press, 2018), pp. 345–82.

La clé du caveau . . . (Paris: Capelle et Renand, 1811).

La famosa contesa tra il busto e la testa della statua di Bruto . . . (Milan: n.n., 1798).

C. Laforte, *Le catalogue de la chanson folklorique française*, vol. 6 (Quebec: La Presse de l'Université Laval, 1983).

P. Landriani, '*Osservazioni sull'Imperial Regio Teatro alla Scala in Milano*', in *Storia e descrizione de' principali teatri antichi e moderni*, ed. by G. Ferrario (Milan: Ferrario, 1830), pp. 257–78.

L'Arciduca Ferdinando spettatore incognito alla gran festa federativa (Milan: n.n., 1797).

J. Livesey, *Making Democracy in the French Revolution* (Cambridge, MA: Harvard University Press, 2001).

P. Lonati, *Description de la fête qui a eu lieu le 10 Floréal an 9 . . .* (Milan: n.n., 1801).

L. Mason, *Singing the French Revolution . . .* (Ithaca: Cornell University Press, 1996).

F. Mastropasqua, *Le feste della Rivoluzione francese: 1790–1794* (Milan: Mursia, 1976).

J. Michelet, *Histoire de la Révolution française*, vol. 2 (Paris: Chamerot, 1847).

A. Mignatti, 'Magnificence and Regality in Milanese Celebratory Sets . . .', in *Magnificence in the Seventeenth Century*, ed. by G. Versteegen, S. Bussels and W. Melion (Leiden: Brill, 2021), pp. 276–307.

Scenari della città (Pisa: F. Serra, 2013), pp. 47–65.

C. Moiraghi, *Napoleone a Milano: 1796–1814* (Bologna: Megalini, 2001).

C. Mozzarelli, '*La Villa, la corte e Milano capitale*', in *La Villa reale di Monza*, ed. by F. De Giacomi (Cinisello Balsamo, Italy: Silvana, 1999), pp. 9–43.

F. Nevola, 'Locating Communities in the Early Modern Italian City', in *Urban History* 37/3 (2010), pp. 349–59.

M. Nocciolini, '*Il melodramma nella Milano napoleonica . . .*', in *Nuova rivista musicale italiana* 29/1 (1995), pp. 5–30.

Notizie storiche e descrizione dell' I. R. Teatro alla Scala (Milan: Salvi, 1856).

Nuovo decadario per l'anno VI della Repubblica francese . . . (Milan: Orena Malatesta, 1798).

A. Ottolini, '*La vita culturale nel periodo napoleonico*', in *Storia di Milano*, ed. by G. Treccani degli Alfieri, vol. 13 (Milan: Fondazione Treccani degli Alfieri, 1956), pp.401–41.

M. Ozouf, *La fête révolutionnaire: 1789–1799* (Paris: Gallimard, 1976).

L'homme régénéré (Paris: Gallimard, 1989).

E. Pagano, *Il Comune di Milano nell'età napoleonica* (Milan: Vita e Pensiero, 1994).

A. Paglicci Brozzi, *Sul teatro giacobino ed antigiacobino in Italia*, vol. 1 (Milan: Pirola, 1887).

F. Palgrave, *Handbook for Travellers in Northern Italy*, 11th ed. (London: J. Murray, 1869).

A. Palidda, '*D'un bel canto patrioto francese . . .*', in *Journal of War & Culture Studies* 14/2 (2021), pp. 175–93.

'*Exsultate, jubilate: musica sacra?*', in *La nostra musica da chiesa è assai differente*, ed. by C. Toscani and R. Mellace (Lucca: SEdM, 2018), pp. 207–26.

'Milan and the Music of Political Transitions in the Napoleonic Period . . .', in *Music and War in Europe from the French Revolution to WWI*, ed. by E. Jardin (Turnhout, Belgium: Brepols, 2016), pp. 105–22.

'*Rediviva sub optimo principe hilaritas publica* . . .', in *Music and Power in the Baroque Era*, ed. by R. Rasch (Turnhout, Belgium: Brepols, 2018), pp. 271–92.

C. Pancera, '*Feste e rituali della rivoluzione*', in *Europa 1700–1992. Storia di una identità*, vol. 2 (Milan: Electa, 1991), pp. 161–71.

G. Panizza and G. Raboni (eds.), *La Milano di Napoleone* . . ., exhibition catalogue, Milan, Biblioteca nazionale Braidense, 5 May–10 July (Milan: Scalpendi, 2021).

G. Parini, *Descrizione delle feste celebrate in Milano per le nozze delle LL. Altezze Reali* . . . (Milan: Società tipografica de' Classici Italiani, 1825).

Poesie (Florence: Barbera, 1808).

N. Parker, *Portrayals of Revolution* (New York: Harvester Wheatsheaf, 1990).

R. Parker, *Arpa d'or dei fatidici vati* . . . (Parma: Istituto Nazionale di Studi Verdiani, 1997).

'On Reading Nineteenth-Century Opera: Verdi through the Looking-Glass,' in *Reading Opera*, ed. by A. Groos and R. Parker (Princeton: Princeton University Press, 1998), pp. 288–305.

R. Paulson, *Images of the Revolution (1789–1820)* (New Haven, CT: Yale University Press, 1983).

C. Pierre, *Les Hymnes et les chansons de la Révolution* (Paris: Imprimerie nationale, 1904).

Musique des fêtes et cérémonies de la Révolution française (Paris: Imprimerie nationale, 1899).

A. Pillepich, *Milan capitale napoléonienne: 1800–1814* (Paris: Lettrage, 2001).

S. Pivato, *Bella ciao. Canto e politica nella storia d'Italia* (Rome: Laterza, 2005).

P. Puppa, '*La coreografia dell'ordine*', *Lo spettacolo nella Rivoluzione francese*, ed. by P. Bosisio (Rome: Bulzoni, 1989), pp. 171–88.

Raccolta degli ordini ed avvisi . . ., vol. 1 (Milan: Veladini, 1796).

A. Ritter von Arneth (ed.), *Briefe der Kaiserin Maria Theresia an ihre Kinder und Freunde*, vol. 1 (Vienna: Braumüller,1881).

Rituel républicain . . . (Paris: Aubry, 1794).

E. Riva, '*La corte dell'arciduca Ferdinando Asburgo Lorena*', in *Il teatro a Milano nel Settecento*, ed. by A. Cascetta and G. Zanlonghi, vol. 1 (Milan: Vita e Pensiero, 2008), pp. 71–96.

M. Robespierre, *Rapport fait au nom du Comité de salut Public . . . sur les Fêtes nationales* (Paris: Quiber-Pallissaux, 1793).

L. Robuschi, *Milano: alla ricerca della città ideale* (Cassina de Pecchi, Italy: Vallardi, 2011).

S. Romagnoli, '*Il Teatro e "Il Caffè"*', in *Economia, istituzioni, cultura in Lombardia nell'età di Maria Teresa*, ed. by A. De Maddalena, E. Rotelli and G. Barbarisi (Bologna: Il Mulino, 1982), pp. 299–318.

J. Rosselli, *The Opera Industry in Italy from Cimarosa to Verdi* (Cambridge: Cambridge University Press, 1984).

E. Rota, '*Milano napoleonica*', in *Storia di Milano*, ed. by G. Treccani degli Alfieri (Milan: Fondazione Treccani degli Alfieri, 1956), pp. 3–348.

G. Salvi, *Scenari di libertà* (Pisa: Serra, 2015).

O. Sanguinetti, *Insorgenze anti-giacobine in Italia (1796–1799)* (Milan: Istituto per la storia delle insorgenze, 2001).

V. Sani, *1799. Napoli. La Rivoluzione* (Venosa, Italy: Osanna, 1799).

R. M. Schafer, 'The Soundscape', in *The Sound Studies Reader*, ed. by J. Sterne (New York: Routledge, 2012), pp. 95–103.

S. Schama, *Rembrandt's Eyes* (New York: Knopf, 1999).

H. Schneider, 'The Sung Constitutions of 1792 . . .' in *Music and the French Revolution*, ed. by M. Boyd (Cambridge: Cambridge University Press, 1992), pp. 236–75.

R. Schober, '*Gli effetti delle riforme di Maria Teresa sulla Lombardia*', in *Economia, istituzioni, cultura in Lombardia . . .*, ed. by A. De Maddalena, E. Rotelli and G. Barbarisi (Bologna: Il Mulino, 1982), pp. 201–14.

A. Scotti Tosini, '*Le trasformazioni della città*', in *Il laboratorio della modernità* (Milan: Skira, 2003), pp. 35–48.

J. C. Sismondi, *A History of the Italian Republics* . . . (London: Longman, 1832).

Sopra il nome di Porta Marenco dato all'antica Porta Ticinese di Milano (Milan: Pirotta e Maspero, 1809).

F. Souchal, *Le vandalisme de la Révolution* (Paris: Novelles Éditions Latines, 1993).

Stendhal (M.-H. Beyle), *La Chartreuse de Parme*, ed. by E. Abravanel (Geneva: Cercle du Bibliophile, 1969).

Storia della fondazione del Lazzaretto fuori di Porta Orientale . . . (Milan: n.n., 1797).

G. Strafforello, *La Patria. Geografia dell'Italia*, ed. by G. Chiesi, vol. 10 (Turin: UTE, 1894).

R. Strohm, *Music in Late Medieval Bruges*, 2nd ed. (Oxford: Clarendon Press, 1990).

F. Sulis, *Dei moti politici dell'isola di Sardegna dal 1793 al 1821* (Turin: Biancardi, 1857).

R. Sweet, *Cities and the Grand Tour* ... (Cambridge: Cambridge University Press, 2012).

Tavole di ragguaglio pel confronto delle date ... (Milan: Borsani, 1805).

G. Tintori (ed.), *Duecento anni alla Scala 1778–1978*, exhibition catalogue, Milan, Palazzo Reale, 16 February–10 September (Milan: Electa, 1978).

G. Tocchini, '*Dall'antico regime alla Cisalpina* ...', in *Salfi librettista*, ed. by F. P. Russo (Vibo Valentia, Italy: Monteleone, 2001), pp. 19–81.

I. Tognarini, '*Le repubbliche giacobine*', in *Storia della società italiana*, ed. by G. Cherubini, vol.13 (Milan: Teti, 1980), pp.59–82.

C. Torre, *Il ritratto di Milano* ..., 3 vols. (Milan: Agnelli, 1674).

C. Toscani, '*Politica culturale e teatro nell'Italia napoleonica* ...', in *L'aere è fosco, il ciel s'imbruna* ..., ed. by F. Passadore and F. Rossi (Venice: Edizioni Fondazione Levi, 2000), pp. 71–98.

'*Soggetti romantici nell'opera italiana del periodo napoleonico*', in *Aspetti dell'opera italiana fra Sette e Ottocento* ..., ed. by G. Salvetti (Lucca: LIM, 1993), pp. 13–70.

M. Traversier, ' *"Transformer la plèbe en peuple". Théâtre et musique à Naples en 1799* ...', in *Annales historiques de la Révolution française* 335 (2004), pp. 37–70.

J. Tulard, *Napoleone. Il mito del salvatore* (Milan: Rusconi, 1989).

A. Valery, *Historical, Literary, and Artistical Travels in Italy* (Paris: Baudry, 1839).

M. Verga, '*Decadenza*', in *Atlante culturale del Risorgimento*, ed. by A. Banti, A. Chiavistelli, L. Mannori and M. Meriggi (Rome: Laterza, 2011), pp. 5–18.

P. Verri, *Storia di Milano* (Milan: Oliva, 1850).

A. Vicinelli, *Il Parini e Brera* (Milan: Ceschina, 1963).

P. Vismara, '*Forme di devozione e vita religiosa tra continuità e rinnovamento*', in *Il teatro a Milano nel Settecento*, ed. by A. Cascetta and G. Zanlonghi, vol. 1 (Milan: Vita e Pensiero, 2008), pp. 55–69.

'*Il sistema della religione cittadina dei milanesi nel Settecento* ...', in *La cultura della rappresentazione nella Milano del Settecento*, ed. by R. Carpani, A. Cascetta and D. Zardin (Rome: Bulzoni, 2010), pp. 45–76.

D. Wiles, *Theatre and Citizenship. The History of a Practice* (Cambridge: Cambridge University Press, 2014).

C. Wysocki, '*Il giovane Mozart e il Conte Firmian*', in *Mozart e i musicisti italiani del suo tempo*, conference proceedings, Rome, 21–2 October 1991, ed. by A. Bini (Lucca: LIM, 1994), pp. 81–8.

A. Young, *Travels in France and Italy during the years 1787, 1788 and 1789*, ed. by T. Okey (London: Dent, 1915).

Acknowledgements

This Element would not have been possible without contributions from and the support of several individuals and institutions, to whom I give my most heartfelt thanks:

- My PhD supervisor, Professor David Wyn Jones, who first glimpsed the relevance of the topic and supported me throughout the research and writing process.
- The librarians at the Conservatorio 'Giuseppe Verdi' of Milan, who granted me unprecedented access to their incredible sources and who treated me with incredible kindness and respect.
- The Biblioteca nazionale Braidense, Biblioteca Ambrosiana, Civica Raccolta delle Stampe 'Achille Bertarelli', Palazzo Moriggia – Museo del Risorgimento of Milan, Biblioteca civica of Monza, Museo internazionale e biblioteca della musica of Bologna, the British Library and the Bibliothèque nationale de France for their support in the research process and authorization to use their images.
- The series editors at Cambridge University Press who have patiently supported the writing of this Element throughout and beyond the uncertain times of the pandemic.

Cambridge Elements ≡

Music and the City

Simon McVeigh

University of London

Simon McVeigh is Professor of Music at Goldsmiths, University of London, and President of the Royal Musical Association. His research focuses on British musical life 1700–1945; and on violin music and performance practices of the period. Books include *Concert Life in London from Mozart to Haydn* (Cambridge) and *The Italian Solo Concerto 1700–1760* (Boydell). Current work centres on London concert life around 1900: a substantial article on the London Symphony Orchestra was published in 2013 and a book exploring London's musical life in the Edwardian era is in preparation for Boydell. He is also co-investigator on the digital concert-programme initiative *InConcert*.

Laudan Nooshin

City University, London

Laudan Nooshin is Professor in Music at City University, London. She has research interests in creative processes in Iranian music; music and youth culture in Iran; urban sound; music in Iranian cinema and music and gender. Her publications include *Iranian Classical Music: The Discourses and Practice of Creativity* (2015, Ashgate, awarded the 2016 British Forum for Ethnomusicology Book Prize); *Music and the Play of Power in the Middle East, North Africa and Central Asia* (ed. 2009, Ashgate) and *The Ethnomusicology of Western Art Music* (ed. 2013, Routledge), as well as numerous journal articles and book chapters. Between 2007 and 2011, Laudan was co-editor of the journal *Ethnomusicology Forum*.

About the Series

Elements in Music and the City sets urban musical cultures within new global and cross-disciplinary perspectives

The series aims to open up new ways of thinking about music in an urban context, embracing the widest diversity of music and sound in cities across the world. Breaking down boundaries between historical and contemporary, and between popular and high art, it seeks to illuminate the diverse urban environment in all its exhilarating and vivid complexity. The urban thus becomes a microcosm of a much messier, yet ultimately much richer, conception of the 'music of everyday life'.

Rigorously peer-reviewed and written by leading scholars in their fields, each Element offers authoritative and challenging approaches towards a fast-developing area of music research. Elements in Music and the City will present extended case-studies within a comparative perspective, while developing pioneering new theoretical frameworks for an emerging field.

The series is inherently cross-disciplinary and global in its perspective, as reflected in the wide-ranging multi-national advisory board. It will encourage a similar diversity of approaches, ranging from the historical and ethnomusicological to contemporary popular music and sound studies.

Written in a clear, engaging style without the need for specialist musical knowledge, *Elements in Music and the City* aims to fill the demand for easily accessible, quality texts available for teaching and research. It will be of interest not only to researchers and students in music and related arts, but also to a broad range of readers intrigued by how we might understand music and sound in its social, cultural and political contexts

Cambridge Elements ≡

Music and the City

Elements in the Series

Popular Music Heritage, Cultural Justice and the Deindustrialising City
Sarah Baker, Zelmarie Cantillon and Raphaël Nowak

Mapping (Post)colonial Paris by Ear
Naomi Waltham-Smith

Music from Aleppo during the Syrian War
Clara Wenz

Urban Spectacle in Republican Milan
Alessandra Palidda

A full series listing is available at: www.cambridge.org/emtc

Printed in the United States
by Baker & Taylor Publisher Services